"There's no other book quite like *The Finance of Romance*. I found it to be refreshingly practical, entertaining, easy-to-read, financially sound, and dead on about romantic love relationships. This is definitely a book that you buy once, and refer to again and again."—*Steve Nakamoto, two-time Writer's Digest award-winning relationship author and The iVillage.com's Mr. Answer Man relationship expert advisor*

"I've seen many books on relationships over the years, but approaching love as you would approach money is not only exciting, but simple and practical. I've never seen anything like *The Finance of Romance*, and I think it will change lives." —*Susan Heim, coauthor, Chicken Soup for the Soul series*

"Romance for men can be scary stuff. Leon's incredible sense of humor and brilliant connection with money makes this a book that all men will actually enjoy reading."—*Michael Webb, bestselling relationship author and founder of TheRomantic.com*

"Talk about growing your investment and reducing risk at the same time. *The Finance of Romance* is a small price to pay to ensure your relationship will grow throughout the years. If only all companies were this conscientious." —*Gary Patterson, The Fiscal Doctor, author,* Stick Out Your Balance Sheet and Cough

"Leon Scott Baxter draws insightful parallels between successfully building a financial portfolio and investing in your love portfolio. Both men and women can benefit from *The Finance of Romance!*"—*Gail Rubin, author,* A Girl's Pocket Guide to Trouser Trout: Reflections on Dating and Fly-Fishing

"As a financial advisor, I find Leon's tips sound and easy to follow. When he correlates the same tips for love, everything comes together. My clients are going to really appreciate and enjoy *The Finance of Romance*."—*Timothy N. Tremblay, OSJ, registered securities principal*

"The analogies between money and relationships were absolutely brilliant in *The Finance of Romance*. The book is packed with insightful information, practical advice and thought-provoking exercises, and is written in a humorous style that made the book an absolute joy to read."—*Talayah Stovall, speaker, life purpose coach, and author,* Crossing the Threshold

"Leon hit the lottery with this book, which takes the approach that investing into your relationship is just as important as how we should manage our bank accounts. Both men and the women they love will benefit from the easy-to-read—and even easier-to-apply—tools and questionnaires that encourage couples to 'bank more bucks' in their love life! All relationships will enjoy and benefit from Leon's wisdom, loving spirit and his heartfelt wish for your success!" —*Dr. Joni Frater & Esther Lastique, authors,* Love Her Right

"As a life coach and radio host, I've seen and read a lot of books on relationships, but nothing like *The Finance of Romance*. It's funny, practical, and easy to apply. Leon Scott Baxter has created the blueprint for family and relationship success! This is one investment you'll be grateful you made."—*Line Brunet, life coach and host of Family Focus Radio Show*

"*The Finance of Romance* is both relevant and thought-provoking; paralleling the importance of finances to relationships is pure genius! While men consider themselves 'financial experts,' women are more often 'communication experts.' America's Romance Guru's sappy sense of humor will keep both men and women smiling page after page as they learn how to connect with each other's 'expertise.'" —*Simon Presland, professional writer and editor*

"*The Finance of Romance* is filled with good advice. It's a fun, easy, and entertaining read. I'm glad I read it. I give it 5 stars and strongly recommend it for anyone who is looking to strengthen his/her relationship."—*Elizabeth Blake, author of the award-winning* No Child Left Behind? The True Story of a Teacher's Quest

"Leon Scott Baxter has written an absolutely outstanding guide for anyone who is married, no matter if they are newlyweds or celebrating 40 years of marriage. The tips at the end of each chapter are priceless and extremely valuable in making anyone's relationship thrive. Just like investing, relationships require we first make deposits before making a withdrawal. Leon shows you all of this in a humorous and easy-to-read format."—*Gary Spinell, self-help/motivation author,* It Was YOU All Along

"You will enjoy reading this book and recognizing that there are tangible rewards for investing in family. Those investments will pay off not just in the future, but right now. Here's to a happy and fulfilled life. Thanks, Leon, for being our guide."—*Judy Helm Wright, speaker on family relationship issues and author,* Using Encouraging Words

"This smart and funny book shows you how to invest in your relationship and get a positive return. Wow, I've already strengthened my relationship portfolio."—*D. E. Boone, author,* Legs Talk: A Modern Girl's Dating Tale

"If you are in a relationship and you care enough about it to keep it strong, healthy, and enjoyable, then buy *The Finance of Romance*! Not only will you find it to be a practical guide to staying on course, but it's also a really fun read, an investment you and your partner won't regret."—*Paul & Debbie Lamb, authors of* Be a Better Partner

"As the owner and operator of several successful dating services in Northern America, I find Leon's approach to relationships refreshingly practical. The work that is involved in finance, or making your fortune, doesn't end at the starting line, and neither do relationships!"—*Paul Goldenberg, former owner of dating services*

# THE
# FINANCE
## OF Romance

INVESTING
IN YOUR
RELATIONSHIP
PORTFOLIO

To J.J. Reed '95
Best to you
both!

# LEON SCOTT BAXTER

LSBaxter

SWEETWATER BOOKS
AN IMPRINT OF CEDAR FORT, INC.
SPRINGVILLE, UTAH

ISBN 13: 978-1-59955-980-3

Published by Sweetwater Books, an imprint of Cedar Fort, Inc.
2373 W. 700 S., Springville, UT 84663
Distributed by Cedar Fort, Inc., www.cedarfort.com

LIBRARY OF CONGRESS CATALOGING-IN-PUBLICATION DATA

Baxter, Leon Scott, 1968- , author.
  The finance of romance / Leon Scott Baxter.
      p. cm.
  Summary: Tips on how to have a successful marriage.
  ISBN 978-1-59955-980-3
  1. Marriage. 2. Man-woman relationships. 3. Finance, Personal. I.
Title.
  HQ734.B29 2011
  306.81--dc23
                              2011040403

Cover design by Brian Halley
Cover design © 2012 by Lyle Mortimer
Edited and typeset by Melissa J. Caldwell

Printed in the United States of America

10  9  8  7  6  5  4  3  2  1

Printed on acid-free paper

*For Lisa,*
*the Monkey and the Raccoon*

# CONTENTS

# FOREWORD

During these difficult economic times, The Finance of Romance is a smart purchase for anyone who understands the importance—and the joy—of investing in a lasting relationship. America's Romance Guru, author Leon Scott Baxter, is uniquely qualified to serve as an advisor for relationship investments. He delivers his message with insight and good humor. What's more, he lives what he teaches.

Long before his wife Mary broke the you're-going-to-be-a daddy news to him, Leon was a well-known romance expert. During her two pregnancies, he worked hard to make Mary feel special and cared for and to adapt to her changing needs. He shared his newfound knowledge in A Labor with Love: A Dad's-to-Be Guide to Romance During Pregnancy. His week-by-week romance suggestions culminate at week 40: shave her legs—something that's been inconvenient if not impossible during her last trimester—before the blessed event. That's a man who knows how to love and pamper his wife, the romance part of the equation.

Leon and Mary invest time, money, and energy in their relationship, and this investment serves as an example for their daughters. They also discuss investing and saving with their children. The impressive thing is that their girls not only listen, they act upon mama and papa's sage advice. Both children put a portion of their allowances into savings. The ten-year-old started her own company three years ago. Maddie's Monkey Business manufactures hand-crafted items like bracelets and picture frames. She pays herself a monthly salary, donates to charity, reinvests in her business, and buys stock. Any man who can inspire his young daughter to choose Intel stock over Barbie dolls understands the financial part of the equation, too.

I'm a long-time believer in the value of investing in relationships. In fact, in The Art of the Spark: 12 Habits to Inspire Romantic Adventures, I wrote a section entitled "Invest in Your Relationship." In the entire book, I devoted only two pages to the topic, which included a simple chart that shows love interest growing with investments of time and money. I hoped that would persuade my readers.

Leon persuades brilliantly by applying sound financial principles to relationships: begin investing today, get rid of debt, change spending habits, invest regularly and diversify, assess risks, maintain good credit, and reinvest profits. No one would doubt the wisdom in this financial advice. With logic and humor, Leon explains the growth potential by investing in your "relationship portfolio." Even small financial sacrifices can result in significant gains. He makes packing a sack lunch sound downright sexy.

Leon sees parallels between finance and romance that make sense. Think about how to maintain good credit. If you pay your bills on time, banks trust you. A credit score reflects your credit worthiness and determines the interest rate you will be charged on loans. In a relationship, you may need to take out a loan from your relationship portfolio if you make a mistake like forgetting a birthday or getting home late. Your credit score determines how much interest your partner will charge you. Interest is the length of time it takes to be forgiven. Leon developed a five-question quiz to determine a relationship credit score, and proposes strategies to rebuild credit. This guy is like the Warren Buffett of romance.

Like any good financial advisor, Leon has you put pencil to paper for portfolio-stretching exercises in each chapter. Instead of financial goals, however, Leon teaches you to explore relationship goals, such as arguing less, being more affectionate, or taking more getaways as a couple. You consider the investments you are willing to make, which can run the gamut from hugs to trips to the Bahamas.

Reading Leon Scott Baxter's The Finance of Romance is like having a conversation with a very funny, very smart, and helpful friend. You'll laugh out loud, but best of all, when you're done reading you will have a solid plan for romance and finance that will pay beautiful dividends throughout your life.

**Mary Zalmanek**
author, *The Art of the Spark:*
*12 Habits to Inspire Romantic Adventures*

# INTRODUCTION

_____

*I*t may come off as a rather strange concept: investing in your relationship portfolio. But, really, it makes sense. We invest financially so that we will be better off down the road than we are today.

The concept behind *The Finance of Romance* is to do the same for our relationships. Invest in them the way we would in businesses, tax-sheltered annuities (TSAs), or in the stock market, so that our relationships grows stronger tomorrow than they are today.

The book you now hold in your hands (unless you have only received just this one page, in which case you are either the butt of a lame joke, or someone really didn't like my book and you have found the remnants of their maniacal tearing spree, either of which should lead you to recycle this one sheet or head over to your local bookstore and purchase the rest of the book) is simply a guide to investing in your future—the future of your relationship. It takes widely popular investment tips from the world's richest people and the most successful financial gurus and shows you how those proven techniques are also appropriate for your relationship.

Simple concept. It allows lots of folks to finally "get it" when it comes to relationships. Those who think logically versus emotionally, concretely versus abstractly, periodically versus frequently will truly benefit from *The Finance of Romance*. And, if I am wrong and they do not benefit from this book, you have my blessing to either tear out this first page and give it to someone as a practical joke or maniacally tear the whole thing up and leave the pages strewn about for others to find and eventually recycle.

Now, on with the show. Please enjoy, and read with your mouth closed . . . for the safety of others.

— CHAPTER ONE —

# WHY YOU NEED TO INVEST

*Love is not what makes the world go 'round. Romance is.*
*And it's my job to keep everyone dizzy.*

*L*et's start with an impromptu survey. If you had the choice, raise your hand if you'd choose all the money you could ever need, but have a lifelong relationship without romance. Take this opportunity to look around the room and count the hands you see.

Now, raise your hand if you would choose a happy, fulfilling, lifelong, romantic relationship with one partner till "death do us part," but with just enough money to get by to meet your basic necessities (maybe a *People Magazine* now and again). Okay, count those who've raised their hands.

What did you notice? Exactly. You were the only one in the room with your arm extended. Was the choice you made kind of tough? Love or money?

We all know deep down that loving relationships are what make us happy in life, but it's hard not to think that money can do the same. I mean, there are studies that show money can't buy happiness,[1] and even John, Paul, George, and Ringo told us that "money can't buy me love."

Now don't get me wrong. I want love, but I wouldn't mind a couple extra Andrew Jacksons in my pocket at the end of the day too. And I'm sure that most of us wouldn't, if the media is any indication. Talk shows, news programs, magazines, websites, books, seminars, articles, DVDs, and more all bombard us with information on finance, saving, and investing.

Now I'm no financial advisor. Instead, I help folks keep the spark in their partnerships alive, the flame of love burning, and the coals of a long-term relationship warm (if not hot). You might think of me as your romantic advisor (as opposed to a financial advisor).

I often equate the work, time, and effort needed to keep a relationship on the right path with the kind of work, time, and effort needed to keep folks on their financial paths. My regular clients can always count on me ending my advice with something along the lines of, "The work you put into your relationship now is an investment that will reap incredible dividends down the road."

One day, the good folks at Ocean Hills Covenant Church in Santa Barbara, California, asked me to speak to their congregation about romance. The focus was to be on balancing marital relationships and parenthood. The talk was to take place after the Sunday sermon to make it convenient for those who wanted to hear me. Immediately, I started work on my discussion, research, presentation, and handouts.

Just so you know, I'm a man with a Type-A personality (maybe A+!). It's not quite a "disorder," but some would argue that medication would help. I get something in my head and that's the way it needs to be. You know how if you pick up a piece of cooked spaghetti, it moves and bends and is flexible? Well, I'm that same piece of spaghetti . . . before it's cooked. Try and wiggle me around, and I *snap*!

So, a few weeks before my talk at Ocean Hills, I received an email from one of the organizers: "Oh, Leon, we've made a few changes . . ."

(Take a deep breath, there, Big Fella.)

"The talk will be on a Saturday evening, rather than a Sunday morning . . ."

(Not so bad. I can handle that.)

"We're changing the location to a loft, a bit more conducive to your talk . . ."

(Hey, this sounds great.)

"It'll be more of an event than just a talk, though. Couples can drop off their children and go to dinner. We'll provide dessert and coffee, and a drawing to attract more folks to the event . . ."

(Wow, this is really shaping up to more than I'd expected.)

"Oh, and by the way, we're allowing anyone to come to this event, not just parents from our congregation. So, if you wouldn't mind opening the topic up to couples in general, we'd appreciate that. Let us know if there's anything you need: water, podium, food, etc. See you in three weeks."

*Snap!* My planning and preparation went out the window. I was traveling down my own path, then I'm asked to turn left at the fork in the road. I'm no good with forks (mashed potato incident of '82), but I had to remind myself of the extra Jacksons in my pocket at the end of the day. Since Ocean Hills was a paying client, I responded back:

"Wow, sounds great. Looking forward to the event. Oh, and I'd love a bottled water. No need for a podium, just a stand. And I'll eat anything but spaghetti. See you soon." (Darn, should have mentioned no mashed potatoes, either.) Turned out, this was the best thing for me. It got me out of my comfort zone and made me think about what angle to take.

Sometimes in life, as in finances and relationships, we need to force ourselves out of our boxes of security so as to grow and reach new goals.

*How could I present the tools for ensuring a happy and successful relationship to an audience from all walks of life, all ages, different eth-nicities, and a variety of economic backgrounds in a way that would interest everyone?* I wondered. Then the light went on. Money. My A+ personality went into high gear and I came up with some financial tips that could be used to parallel a relationship portfolio.

The talk was an incredible success. People took notes and laughed in all the right spots, then thanked me wholeheartedly afterward. The interesting thing was that, unlike my previous talks, workshops, and seminars, more *men* approached and thanked me afterward than women.

*Why?* I asked myself. Then it dawned on me. Men often have trouble wrapping their heads (and hearts) around the abstract concepts involved with love, relationships, and emotions. But when it comes to money, saving, investing, and finance, men tend to feel much more capable. We men can envision how to be successful. We see the growth potential. We understand how we will benefit from solid financial planning down the road. We "get" the finite, concrete steps involved in financial planning. We tend to be more emotionally involved than women when it comes to investments.

When I drew parallels between money and romance, guys saw there were definite steps to create success in the area of relationships. When they saw that there was actual growth potential, when they understood the personal benefits with their partners, their jobs, and their families, they were able to finally relate and hop on board the "relationship" train. That's when it became exciting, and that's when I hit myself in the head with an open palm (not too hard, mind you . . . really just for effect) and decided to write *The Finance of Romance*.

Here are some rules that will help you not only financially, but also in your relationship:

To get what you want, you need to know what you want—today, short-term, long-term, and the retirement years.

To reach these goals you need to communicate with your partner, do some research, attend seminars, and read up on the subject.

It takes work, time, effort, dedication, and sacrifice.

Too many folks wait too long. They expect that everything will either "fall into place" on its own, or they'll worry about it in the future. And, far too often, their goals are never reached.

Those who invest regularly look back at what they've done, where they started, and what they've accomplished and are glad they did it. They also wonder why they didn't start earlier.

So, how can a book like *The Finance of Romance* help you? Because, keeping romance alive is tough for most of us. When we begin dating or courting, or when we're first married, romance, our relationships, and our partners tend to be on the top of our priority lists. But as time goes by and we become more comfortable with the relationships and our partners, we tend to find our relationships moving lower and lower on our priority lists:

1. Family
2. Work
3. Chores
4. Bills
5. Health
6. String cheese
7. Molly Ringwold movies
8. Thursday Night NBC prime time TV shows
9. Coupon clipping
10. The Senate race
11. Taxidermy
12. Spouse

The reason is really not all that nefarious. At the start of a relationship, there's fear that it may not last. So we naturally invest time and resources into keeping it afloat. But as time goes by and we realize that this relationship is going to stick around, we feel okay leaving it to fend for itself at times, because we know it'll be there tomorrow. In other words, we tend to take our relationships for granted.

Is that a problem? Yes, because 41 percent of first marriages in America end in divorce (even higher for second and third marriages[2]). And none of those broken marriages started with divorce as a goal. Neglecting our relationships is a dangerous game of roulette. *I don't need to worry about our relationship. We love each other, and love is enough*, you may think. That's a gamble that rarely pays off.

## Love Is Enough

Let me tell you a little about my youth. My folks divorced when I was six years old. They were in love with one another, but they just didn't get along. Oh yes, we can love and not get along. It happens all the time in families to siblings, a crazy cousin, parents, and teens. Happens in love relationships too. My parents just couldn't connect romantically.

Within two years of the divorce, both my mom and dad were remarried . . . to each other! Yes, that's right; my folks married, divorced, and married one another for a second go-round. It was like one of those games at the carnival. You plunk down five bucks, throw three balls at the plates, miss them all, and walk away feeling dejected and used, and as though you wasted your time and money. You vow never to succumb to the lure of a stuffed St. Bernard toy again. When you get to the cotton candy stand, you think about it and say to yourself, *I can do this. Let me give it one more shot,* and you storm right back over, plunk down another five, and get handed three more balls.

These were my folks, they'd thought about their relationship by the cotton candy stand and said, "We're in love. We can do this!" Then were handed three more balls.

Well, with balls in hand and love in their hearts—God bless their efforts—my folks still couldn't connect. They threw those balls of love at the plates, but there was still no romance in their relationship. Instead, it was full of bickering and arguing.

Coming home from school each day was like a crapshoot for me. Would we have peace or World War III tonight? Walking on eggshells each day can make it easy for a Type-A kid who is looking for structure, order, and a regular routine to "snap."

So, I learned at a very early age that songs like "Love Will Keep Us Together" and "All You Need Is Love" sounded great on the radio but were not very good relationship advice.

Think of it this way: just as making a lot of money alone is not enough to ensure financial security down the road (or even immediately), love by itself is not enough to keep a relationship together, happy, and committed (in most cases).

Financially, you need to plan how to use your money so there will still be something to pull from later on. You need to make and maintain a budget. You need to monitor your spending. And you need to invest. Too often people assume that if they have love, they have a great relationship; it's the same mistake they make when they assume that having a lot of money means they must be rich. These same people could be paid a million dollars a year and still be in debt, just as they could love their spouse, but be on the verge of a divorce.

In a relationship you need to have romance. Love is absolutely crucial, just as money is necessary in financial planning. You need to have something to play with—love or money (depending on what you are investing in). Love is the foundation of all great relationships, but now you have to figure out how to build on it, and romance will give you the biggest return on your investment.

Love is the match that lights the flame. But romance is the oxygen that keeps that flame lit.

So what exactly is romance? Romance is more than loving and caring for your partner. Romance is making your partner *feel* loved and cared for. There's a big difference. Love is what you are "in," but true romance is getting your partner to feel a certain way, based on your actions. What you do is secondary to the results that they produce. Romance is not defined by your actions; it's defined by what your actions produce in your partner. And eliciting emotions of feeling loved or cared for differs for each person.

I remember reading that when Angelina Jolie and Billy Bob Thornton were married, they exchanged vials of blood that they wore around their necks. That wouldn't cut it for me and my wife romantically, but it worked for them. (I'm pretty sure that Count and Countess Dracula, as well as the southwestern water mosquitoes of lower Montana, have also expressed their love in this manner.)

⁂

I'm sure by now you are aware that the goal of this book is to get your relationship back at the top of your priority list and help you keep it there. To do so, you'll find a "Portfolio-Stretching Exercise" at the end of each chapter for you and your partner to work on. Find some time when you two can focus on this activity together. It will help to bring home the ideas from the chapter, while building your relationship portfolio. Here is an example:

## *Portfolio-Stretching Exercise* ———————

1. Look over this list with your partner:

| | |
|---|---|
| *Bills* | *Exercise/Going to the Gym* |
| *Household Chores* | *Finance/ Saving/ Investing* |
| *Faith/Religion/Church* | *Friends* |
| *The Kids* | *Education* |
| *Work* | *Nutrition/Health* |
| *Your Partner/Relationship* | *Charities/Volunteering* |
| *Family* | *Travel* |

2. On your own sheets of paper, separately (maybe even in separate rooms) pick five to eight of these items that you think are currently at the top of your priority list for *this week* (not what you would like to be up there, but what really is there), and rank them from most important to least important. (If you think of an area of importance not listed above, feel free to add it.) Be painfully honest; if not, this exercise will not work. Title this paper, "My Top Priorities This Week." Date it and sign your name. Your partner will do the same (see Worksheet 1).

3. On the back of your sheet, do the same thing as you did in step number two, but this time list the top five to eight categories you think would be your *ideal* priorities in a perfect world. Again, rank them in order, starting with the most important. Label this list, "My Ideal Top Priorities" (see Worksheet 2).

4. Before coming back together, compare your two lists. What differences do you see? What's at the top of this week, and what really should be there? Where does your relationship rank on the two lists? Are you happy with this? What would you like to change? How can you accomplish this? Take notes as you answer these questions.

5. Come back together with your partner and share your first list for this week. Don't discuss the second list just yet. Discuss where your frustrations lie. Let your partner do the same. Are your lists similar in any ways? How are they different?

6. Now, look at your *Ideal* lists. Do your top three match (or come close to) your partner's? Discuss why these are your ideal priorities. Look at your notes. Explain your frustrations and what you believe needs to happen to make this list a reality. Allow your partner to do the same.

7. Come up with an ideal top five list for you as a couple. There may have to be some compromise, which is terrific practice, because we must compromise at times in our relationships. Look at your lists and try to reach a consensus. Write up a

new list. Below the list, bullet three to five ways to make these categories priorities. Post the list on the refrigerator, bathroom mirror, front door, or wherever you both can see it easily every day. Work your behinds off to make these a reality (see Worksheets 1, 2, & 3).

## Key Points for Investing: What You Need to Invest

✓ Set short- and long-term goals.

✓ Research as a team.

✓ Be willing to sacrifice a little.

✓ Don't wait.

✓ Invest regularly into your portfolio.

✓ Invest today and reap the benefits tomorrow.

✓ Love alone is not enough.

✓ Romance creates the biggest return for your investment.

### Notes

1. Australian researcher, Liz Eckermann from Deakin University interviewed 23,000 people.
2. According to http://www.divorcerate.org.

— Chapter Two —

# BEGIN INVESTING TODAY

$\mathcal{L}$ook at the title of this chapter. If you aren't already putting away a few bucks, any financial advisor who knows the basics will say these words to you (again, refer back to the chapter title). And if he doesn't, report him to . . . whatever bureau or commission that regulates financial advisors, because anyone who doesn't tell you to *begin today* isn't worth his weight in shoelaces.

"Put your money in CDs, an IRA, stocks, mutual funds, or real estate. Bear market or bull. Do not wait!" he will tell you. Do it now. Do it today. Start investing right away. A financial advisor friend of mine is known to say, "The best time to start investing was thirty years ago. The second best time is today." Every day you wait is another day lost when building your financial portfolio.

It's funny—young people often assume that it's too early to think about their financial futures. "That's for old people, established folks, people with mortgages, dental plans, and careers (not jobs)." Many of these young people are waiting for "the sign," the *obvious* event sent from the heavens that will put them on the path to investing. But time has a way of sneaking up on us all, and we don't even notice at first. I know I didn't. I was too busy watching episodes of *The A-Team*. But as our incomes and receding hairlines grow, so do our financial responsibilities. Rarely does the obvious celestial event make itself seen, unless we hit it big in Vegas or on a game show, or we win the lottery . . . see chapter thirteen.

Next thing they know, many of these young people find themselves not so young with a mortgage, a dental plan, a receding hairline, and an empty financial portfolio, wishing they'd started years before, even with a small investment.

Money is not just something we spend today and hope more will magically appear tomorrow. Too many of us have forgotten the power of delayed gratification. Money is something we need to use to make more, something to cultivate, so we can harvest during our later years.

I hate to admit it, but I do enjoy catching a reality show on TV now and again. Recently, I saw one in which a woman wanted to date a man, but first his mom would get to look through a file the producers had created, digging up any dirt on the potential date that they could. The woman was in her early twenties and had already accumulated over an eighth of a million dollars in debt. It wasn't school loans or a home purchase; she simply said she liked to shop. Neiman Marcus was an outlet for her. She typifies many of us: we neglect to think about the future, rather finding fulfillment in the immediate, the here and now, because who knows what will happen in the "there and later?"

Like money your relationship is something that you need to get into the habit of investing in (if you're not already)—now, today, the moment you put this book down. Like money, if you don't start investing now, you could find yourself down the road with no growth in your relationship portfolio, and in major debt romantically.

## Resolutions

Were you one of the 50 percent of folks who made a New Year's Resolution this year?[1] If you were—and if you're not reading this during the first week of January—odds are you've already failed to keep your resolution. You've thrown in the towel and have told yourself you'll try again next year. I'm in this negative 50 percent bracket. That's right; I'm right back watching *The A-Team* again on the Internet. It's often easier just to say, "I'll shoot for it again next January."

Here are some interesting stats:

- By February, 50 percent of people who have made a resolution have already abandoned it.[2]
- By year's end, only 8 percent will have kept their resolutions.[3]

With stats like that, the media has been sending a new message lately. Two weeks before the end of the year, magazine articles start popping up, and TV talk shows experts start to preach about the benefits of getting rid of resolutions altogether. (How does one become a resolution expert, by the way? Is there a degree? What kind of education would one need? Just wondering, in case this Romance Guru thing falls through.)

"Odds are, you'll fail," they tell us. Ninety-two percent of us do! So why set yourself up for almost certain failure? It's bad for your self-esteem, psyche, motivation, and ego. You rarely reach your goal. Then, you're right back where you started, but feeling like a schmuck on top of it all, because you hit the gym only twice in six weeks.

Are these "experts" out of their minds? I disagree with these degree-toting, Internet-educated, resolution experts we see on MSNBC. Why? Because they're screaming the mantra, "Give up because it's hard. Give up because it's hard." To quote Nell Carter, "Give me a break."

So you do something that's difficult; you couldn't do it the first time. Big deal. Who taught you to give up after, oh, let's see . . . one time? Not your parents. Not your teachers (unless, of course you had heartless parents and cruel teachers, in which case, I'd understand where you're coming from). And I know it wasn't the self-made industrialist and former president of IBM, Thomas J. Watson. He once said: "Would you like me to give you the formula for success? It's quite simple, really. Double your rate of failure. You are thinking of failure as the enemy of success. But, it isn't at all. You can be discouraged by failure or you can learn from it. So, go ahead and make mistakes. Make all you can. Because, remember, that's where you will find success."

When I was in grade school, I was on a softball team called the Bears. We were a fair team, but the Tigers were ferocious. We'd played them ten times over the previous three years and only out-scored them once. I remember our coach, Gerry Louis (isn't that a kick? Sounds familiar, but spelled differently), telling us we would be playing them for the eleventh time. If you looked at our track record, odds were we were in for another spanking. But not one of the kids on the Bears suggested we forfeit:

"Hey Coach, we've lost 90 percent of our games against the Tigers. If we lose again, won't that affect our self-esteem, psyches, motivation, and egos? Shouldn't we all just call in sick?"

We wouldn't accept that from our children. And I say we don't accept it from the media, and especially not from ourselves. We get knocked down, we jump right back up and give it another go. (By the way, we got spanked again, but we were standing with pride when we took our beating.)

You cheat a little on your resolution. You eat that extra slice of strawberry cheesecake. You smoke half a pack of Marlboros on your "no smoke" day. You skip the gym for a week. Instead of tossing out the resolution altogether, maybe all you need to do is tweak it or readjust the alignment. Instead of only eating sweets once a week, you eat sweets three times a week. Rather than having "no smoke" days, you allow yourself two cigarettes per day all week long. Maybe you don't need to hit the gym every day, but rather every other day and walk thirty minutes in your neighborhood on your days off.

The beauty of resolutions is they are not set in stone and you can *always* reinstate them if you falter. I use the word "always" loosely here. (You wouldn't want to reinstate a resolution during a bris or in the middle of a planned colonoscopy). Most of us associate resolutions with New Year's Day. But a resolution is nothing more than a promise that you make to yourself to do something. The definition has nothing to do with January, the first of the month, nor a new year.

You can resolve to make changes in your life any month, any week, any hour of any day. So, look at the calendar . . . right now. I'll wait.

What event is coming up? Valentine's Day, your birthday,

wedding anniversary, Halloween, Arbor Day? Pick an event to start your resolution (for example, "Your Thanksgiving Resolution"). If nothing's coming up, don't use that as an excuse to put off your resolution. Don't wait for a special day. Create your own: your Wednesday Resolution or the Weekend Resolution.

## *Your* Resolution

What kind of resolution is your romance advisor advocating? I want you to resolve to resurrect the love and romance in your relationship. Do you remember the spark in your relationship when you and your partner first met and dated, or when you were newlyweds? That's what I want you to resolve to reignite.

Like all good resolutions, you must be specific, precise, and make it measurable. You don't *say*, "I want to lose forty pounds by the end of the year." Instead you *write down*, "I will only eat fast food once a week. I'll have at least one salad a day. I will drink six glasses of water a day. I will exercise at least thirty minutes a day, three days a week." The difference is you *write*, you don't *say*. Use statements like, "I will" instead of "I want to," and choose specific actions that you can measure.

As you read the rest of this book, jot down ideas for your resolution so you may whittle down the statement, "I will be more romantic" into specific, precise, measurable steps that will lead you to your goal. But realize, like any true resolution, this will take effort, determination, and work.

I recall a conversation I had with a colleague of mine, Michael, at a grade school where I was teaching in the 1990s. We were discussing this very topic.

"Why would my wife and I want to put out all the work and effort just to reignite that spark?" he asked.

"What do you mean?" I responded, genuinely dumbfounded. "It's romance. It's your relationship. It's your wife."

"Yeah, but what if we're content with how things are now?"

Michael went on to point out that neither he nor his wife longed for those giddy, high school emotions of yesteryear, the passion of courting, the excitement of being newlyweds.

"If we're comfortable with our relationship now—the calm, the content—why should we feel the pressure of bringing romance back to it? Why do the work if neither of us longs to regain what we've lost?"

I just stood there, smiling like an ass (just so we're all on the same page, I'm referring to the animal, a smiling animal), because no one had ever asked me anything like that before. It had always been, "We miss the passion. How do we get it back?" or "What tricks can you teach us to help ignite our flame?" Never had anyone asked, "Why? Why do we need romance?"

First of all, I thought the man—and his wife, if she too was fine without romance—must be completely bonkers. I understand that my response was based on my bias, because I truly look forward to falling in love with my wife again. Mind you, I don't have the time or the energy to be infatuated, passionate, and excited about her 24/7. But every couple of months or so, I find myself longing to spend more time with her, to touch her, to joke around with her. I find myself buying flowers on my way out of the grocery store (who wouldn't want grocery store daisies, eh?), or typing her a quick email.

This, to me, is falling in love again with my wife. It brings me back to years gone by. It makes me happy. I feel younger and it's fun. It reminds me of the days of a full head of hair and B. A. Baracus intimidating bad guys on *The A-Team*. How could Michael and his wife be fine with the loss of this very important part of their lives?

My assumption: they just forgot how it felt, what it was like. Kind of like chocolate. Can you imagine someone telling you, "Oh, no, we don't eat chocolate anymore; it keeps us awake, makes us break out, gives is cavities, and adds on the pounds. Why would we want to take the time and effort to eat it?"

Because it tastes so bloody good! My guess is after one bite, they'd say, "Oh yes, now we remember. This stuff is good. We'll take fourteen pounds, please."

If Michael had tasted romance once again, falling back in love, the passion, and excitement, he would say, "Ah yes. Now I remember. It's been so long. Good stuff, good stuff. I'll take fourteen pounds, please."

But Michael never did get another taste. And with me being a brittle strand of spaghetti (figuratively speaking, of course, because in reality I'm more of a rigatoni), unwilling to relinquish a battle and accept a loss, I answered his, "Why work on love?" question from a different angle.

"If you don't care about regaining the feelings," I explained, "just think about the other benefits associated with being half of a loving and romantic partnership."

See, when you get back those feelings of passion and excitement, we call that the "honeymoon stage." (I'll explain more in depth in chapter seven). Doctors and scientists have found that brain chemistry differs from nearly every other time in life during this stage (save for the times you may have been addicted to narcotics in the mid 90s).[4] As a result of the hormones and chemicals being released during the honeymoon stage, your brain and body reward you.

"How?" you may ask. Well, the men and women in the funny white lab coats, wearing latex gloves and looking at Petri dishes, into microscopes, and at the results of EKGs, EEGs, and ESPN have found that some of the benefits[5] of experiencing a consistently romantic relationship include

- Increased energy
- Decreased anxiety and worry
- More productivity at work and projects
- Overall better health and fitness
- A sense of happiness and contentment
- The aging process appearing to slow down
- Being sick less often
- A stronger family foundation

After relaying this list to Michael, he just nodded and looked away in silence for a good twenty seconds. When his eyes returned to mine, he asked, "So how do you go about teaching indirect objects in your class?" The topic was never broached again. (By the way, because indirect objects were tough for me, I just never told the students they existed. As a result, they were never able to use sentences like: I shall make my grandmother a chocolate soufflé.)

My point is *start now*; begin to fan the flame of romance now, because the changes romance makes within us affect our brain chemistry in a positive way, which can affect aspects of our lives other than just our relationships.

# *Portfolio-Stretching Exercise*
(See Worksheets 4 and 5)

1. Separately, you and your partner should decide on an area within your relationship that needs improving. Please do not pick something that you feel your partner struggles with. Choose either something you both need to work on together, or an area in which you think *you* could improve. Here are some examples:

   - *Spend time together more often.*
   - *Argue less.*
   - *Be more affectionate.*
   - *Be more romantic.*
   - *Become more spontaneous.*
   - *Make sex exciting again.*
   - *Take more getaways as a couple.*

2. Whatever you decide, write it down. This is your relationship goal.

3. Next, still separate from one another, develop three different ideas that will help lead you to your goal. To help you do this, first look at what has been keeping you from reaching your goal. What obstacles have hindered your progress in the past? What three methods can you use to accomplish your relationship goal? Write them down.

4. Now choose one of these three methods, the one you most believe you can truly utilize more easily than the other two. Once you've done this, it's time to write your resolution. Please write it in the following format:

   *"I want to (your goal), therefore I resolve that I will (your method) [and be sure it includes a time frame]."*

   **Examples:**

   "I want to be more affectionate with my husband, therefore I resolve to kiss him at least five times a day, as well as hug him at least five times daily."

"I want to take more getaways with my wife, therefore I resolve to leave one weekend open each month for an out-of-town, over-night trip (to be determined jointly each month)."

5. Be sure to keep your other two methods handy—on the back of the page where you just wrote your resolution is a good spot—in case you find your first plan of action too difficult or not realistic, or it becomes monotonous down the line. This will give you two other paths in which to reach the same destination.

6. Go to the nearest calendar and find a holiday, event, or national week (for example, National "Shave Your Hamster" Week), and name your resolution appropriately: "My Flag Day Resolution." If the calendar is blank the week you choose, name your resolution after a day of the week: "My Tuesday Resolution." Write your resolution name at the top of your page and start your resolution on the corresponding day.

7. Come back together and share your goals with each other, the "I want to argue less" part of your resolution. And, if you like, you can also share your method of reaching this goal. You may also want to share the entire resolution because your partner may be an integral part of making it happen, it can't happen unless they are in on it, or you may want the moral support of your partner to help inspire you to keep the resolution. Some may want to keep the method to themselves because they plan to surprise their partner, or they may feel too vulnerable, fearing scrutiny from their partner should they fall short on their resolution.

## *Key Points for Investing:*
## *Begin Investing Today*

✓ Start right away.

✓ Make a resolution.

✓ Be specific about your goal.

✓ Write it down.

✓ Stick with it even when you stumble.

✓ The benefits are bountiful.

## Notes

1. According to realscienceofsuccess.com, 50 percent of Americans make New Year's Resolutions.

2. "Press Release," Big White Wall, January 2008, http://www.bigwhitewall .com/useful-stuff/PRESS-RELEASE-New-Years-Resolution-Have-a -healthy-head-and-the-rest-will-follow/.

3. "Ninety-two Percent of New Year's Resolutions Won't Be Kept," December 2005, http://www.pr9.net/games/consumer/3207december. html.

4. Neely Tucker, "An Affair of the Head," *Washington Post*, February 13, 2007, http://www.washingtonpost.com/wp-dyn/content/article/2007/02/12/ AR2007021201657.html.

5. M. Langton, "The Health Benefits of Love," November 13, 2007, http:// www.associatedcontent.com/article/443851/the_health_benefits_of_ love.html?cat=5; Sarah Mahoney, MSN/*Prevention Magazine*, "How Love Keeps Us Healthy," http://www.health.msn.com/womens-health/ articlepage.aspx?cp-documentid=100123218&GT1=7756; and Rachel Day, Nine MSN, "The Health Benefits of Love," February 11, 2008, http://www.health.ninemsn.com.au/article.aspx?id=378472.

# Chapter Three

# GET RID
# OF YOUR DEBT

So, let's say one day you decide it's important to start saving for the future, to put away a little each month, to open a CD, to invest in a mutual fund. You start making 4 percent, 7 percent, maybe 12 percent on your money, and you feel good about it. Using newly acquired yoga techniques, you pat yourself on the back and give yourself a hearty, "Atta boy." Then someone points out your credit card debt. You're paying 23 percent on your Citibank Visa, but doing backflips over your 12 percent return on your Oppenheimer Mutual Fund.

The reality is you are losing money! Let me show you. We'll look at $200.

## Scenario #1

You owe $100 on your credit card, and you keep the balance all year, which costs you $23 with an annual interest rate of 23%. The other c-note you're earning twelve bucks a year, with the interest you're getting on your mutual fund. That's a $12 gain and a $23 loss, for a grand total of eleven bucks down the toilet (now who's doing back-flips?).

My dear friend, to be able to you reap the benefits of investing, you must clear out as much debt as possible.

## Scenario #2

You take your second $100 and you pay off your credit card. Sure, you're not making a red cent in interest, but neither are you paying any interest . . . for a grand total of zero dollars (which, by the way, is eleven more dollars than scenario #1).

Once you have eliminated your debt, you are able to take new-found cash and start investing it, reaping a positive return without any nagging interest to pay, which always seems to take the wind out of anyone's financial sails.

You can't build wealth if you are in debt. The same holds true for relationships. You can't build a relationship portfolio if your relationship is in debt. You can go on dates, buy your partner gifts, write him or her love notes, take trips, but it will all be fruitless (like a 12 percent return) if your relationship is in debt (23 percent annually).

## Relationship Debt

What is debt in a relationship? Debt is anything that takes away from allowing you to invest fully. In other words, if the negative outweighs the positive, you will be losing ground no matter what you do, until you deal with your debt.

Debt can include, but is not limited to, spats over money, anger issues, infidelity, mistrust and distrust, emotional isolation, nagging, backbiting, and more.

What do you do about these types of debts? You can't hide from them or pretend they aren't there. You can't put a bandage on them and hope a love poem and a foot rub will make them go away; they won't.

You need to pay off your debt in full and get to a zero balance, before you can start building your portfolio. The truth of the matter is that it's a lot more fun to invest and a lot less pleasurable to pay off your debt. You feel more fulfilled in the short run when you sock away a few bucks into our IRA. You feel good about yourselves right away. Endorphins start flowing, and you're back to yoga-reaching back-patting. But the pleasure is short lived, because you're reminded of your debt when that credit card bill rears its ugly envelope-shaped head in your mailbox at the end of the month. Guilt replaces endorphins. You get depressed and upset with yourself. So what do you do to feel better? Charge something on the card.

If you know you have a marital issue that isn't resolved in twenty-four hours; if you avoid a topic because you know it will bring out the ugly in at least one of you; if there's a giant elephant in the room that you are both pretending is not there, you'll feel good temporarily when you go out together to a concert, endorphins flowing, smiling like the beginning of each *Fantasy Island* episode. But when someone finally steps in that pachyderm poop, you'll be right back to the Blame Game again. Frustration, guilt, and even anger take over where endorphins once ruled, and the wrath-of-Kahn-like look bleeds through your eyes—or your partner's—again.

You need to deal with the issues before you can build that port-folio. How do you do it? First things first: you communicate. I know it sounds easy on paper, but it can be tough, especially if you're dealing with infidelity or trust issues.

## Talk about It

It can feel as though keeping these things hidden and bottled up is the best for the relationship. If you avoid the problem, you have no problem. But this isn't true. If you avoid your debt, no matter how nice your car is or how expensive your clothes are, it may look swell from the outside, you'll have to pay for it at the end of the month. Debt—financial or marital—always weighs heavily on a relationship over time.

So talk. Sit down and talk about your problems. Yes, it may get uncomfortable at some point, but once you air your dirty laundry, you've got that fresh-from-the-outdoors scent on all your unmentionables. In other words, it gets much easier to deal with the issues and talk about them if everyone knows what they are. (Note: I didn't say yell, scream, and blame. I said *t-a-l-k* about your issues.)

So, how do you discuss your debt without compounding it? You need to be civil, avoid attacking, and don't become defensive. I'll admit, this is not always easy, but if you don't allow your feelings to rule your words, you'll both be better off in the long run. You'll want to use "I" statements instead of "you" statements. For example:

*"I still feel hurt that you didn't tell me that you lost our rent playing craps in Atlantic City in February"* **versus** *"You always waste our money without talking to me, like the time you lost our rent money in Atlantic City."*

The first statement is about you and your feelings. The second one is a direct attack on your partner and is guaranteed to put him or her on the defensive. They *will* attack back. You will increase your debt, and you will be farther from your goal of a zero balance than before you started.

❧

I know a couple, Thomas and Lynn, who, for all accounts, seemed like a happy couple. They would go to the movies. He'd surprise her with flowers. She'd cook his favorite meals. They would kiss and hug one another out in public. Married twelve years, they appeared to be building their romantic portfolio. But, in actuality, they were in severe relationship debt.

Drinking and physical abuse occurred regularly in their household. When they drank, abuse would invariably follow. During these times, yelling and arguing, crying, name-calling, and attacks would fill the house. When they sobered up, Thomas and Lynn would be their 12 percent return on investment, but they never attempted to deal with their debt. When times were "good," they were leery that things could go awry at any moment.

I asked Lynn why she never dealt with the problem. Her answer: "When we fight it's so bad that when we're not fighting, I want to enjoy it as long as I can." She knew it wouldn't last forever.

I asked Thomas the same question. "I feel guilty about what I do, and something inside of me partly hopes that if I don't mention it, Lynn will forget it." Which, of course, she can't.

How did this love story end? Six years later, Thomas was out of the house and Lynn was dating another man. Funny thing—or sad, depending on how you look at it—the two loved each other, really loved each other, but love wasn't enough. You need romance, but to build that portfolio is virtually impossible if you are in relationship debt.

## Need More Help?

What do you do if you can't get out of debt on your own? As with your finances, you need to find a professional in relationships, such as a couples therapist or a marriage counselor (see Chapter 11, "Is It Time to Hire a Professional?").

The US Department of Labor puts out a retirement savings education booklet called *Savings Fitness: A Guide to Your Money and Your Financial Future* to help folks deal with finances. On the topic of financial planners, the booklet states that a professional planner can

- provide expertise you don't have
- help improve your current financial management
- save you time
- provide an objective perspective
- help you through a financial crisis
- motivate you to take action[1]

I look at this list and see many parallels to a marriage therapist. A couple's therapist can

- provide expertise you don't have
- help improve your current relationship status
- save you time
- provide an objective perspective
- help you through a relationship crisis
- motivate you to take action

You and your partner are ultimately responsible for your relationship, but sometimes you need someone to guide you, someone who can see the big picture. Some couples, and individuals for that matter, may feel ashamed or embarrassed at the thought of needing to rely on an "outsider" to help them conquer the difficulties in their relationships. But it's nothing to be ashamed of. Each year hundreds of thousands of couples enter into counseling to patch up holes in their relationships.[2] And without said "patches," many would end up deeper in debt or possibly in relationship bankruptcy, separated, or divorced.

If you think of the financial parallel again, according to Tim

Tremblay, Registered Securities Principal of Tremblay Financial, people who go to financial seminars have a net value of 20 percent more than those who don't. In other words, those who seek help have more success than those who do not. The parallel extends to relationships, especially those in debt. Couples who struggle to climb out of the hole on their own are more successful in their relationships after receiving counseling than couples that haven't.

"What if my partner refuses to get help with me?" Go alone. You can still get expert opinion, motivation, and an objective point of view. Your professional can give you tips you can utilize on your own, offer you techniques to improve communication, or even help to inspire your partner to join you at some point.

When you finally have your debt under control, what do you do next? Cut up your credit cards and avoid charging again like the plague. (In other words, don't fall back into relationship debt!) Disagreements are fine, but quickly get them out in the open. Communicate. Resolve issues and move forward. By all means, be trustworthy and faithful. And going to a counselor now and again for a check up (you wouldn't bail on the financial planner who put you on the right track, would you?) is a great idea.

## Portfolio-Stretching Exercise

Are you and your partner in relationship debt? Remember, even if you think your relationship is debt-free, if your partner is carrying debt, the whole relationship has a negative balance.

1. Both you and your partner take a pen and paper and head to a different room. Here you will do some deep and serious thinking. Is there debt in your relationship? Think about obstacles that might be hindering your relationship from progressing, or blocking the two of you from feeling closer. We're not talking about the little things here, like his inability to wash dishes properly or her leaving the bathroom light on—unless these are issues that really are causing debt in your relationship. More often we're staring at the elephant in the

room: the addictions, the lying, the sneakiness, the substance abuse, the infidelity, the physical or verbal abuse, the loss of trust, and so on.

We're looking at issues that you always seem to find your way back to—issues that, when brought up, cause guilt, anger, frustration, tears, or yelling. If these exist in your relationship, write them down.

When you come back together in step number 7, it may be a couple of days from when you first started this exercise.

2. If neither you nor your partner has written anything down, consider your relationship debt free. (Hopefully, you are both being honest). You are now able to move forward in building your relationship portfolio. Feel free to move on to the next chapter.

3. If either you or your partner have written down one or more obstacles in your relationship, alongside each one, list the feelings you associate with those obstacles, emotions you have when you think about them, and feelings that emerge when you and your partner "discuss" them (see Worksheet 6). Feel free to make copies of this list for both you and your partner:

| | | | | |
|---|---|---|---|---|
| *anger* | *sadness* | *frustration* | *guilt* | *abandonment* |
| *abused* | *fear* | *aggravation* | *loneliness* | *beaten down* |
| *bitterness* | *boiling* | *broken* | *furious* | *fuming* |
| *frigid* | *disturbed* | *stress* | *disgust* | *despondent* |
| *depressed* | *confusion* | *gnawing* | *haggard* | *hardened* |
| *heavy* | *hurt* | *intimidation* | *irrational* | *jealousy* |
| *lost* | *melancholy* | *nervousness* | *shame* | *shaken* |
| *seething* | *resigned* | *resentment* | *rejection* | *provoked* |
| *pressure* | *plagued* | *numb* | *stranded* | *uncomfortable* |
| *stunned* | *threatened* | *troubled* | *vulnerable* | *unfeeling* |
| *stung* | *taken advantage of* | | | |

4. Take a separate sheet of paper for each of the obstacles you listed in step #1. On top write the obstacle that's causing debt.

**Example:** "The affair he/she had three years ago"

Then write everything you want to say to your partner about it. Don't worry; they will not see this. This is an opportunity to say what you really feel. You don't need to be politically correct here. You can write what you've been afraid (or not afraid) to say. All of the debt that's been weighing you and your relationship down can now be lifted off your shoulders. It's time to get everything off your chest. Clear your mind. And any other body analogy you can think of.

You may get angry or cry as you write. Let that happen. These may be feelings you've bottled up for some time. Get that elephant out of the room and on that paper. Don't worry about spelling or sentence structure or hurting anyone's feelings. This is about you right now.

You can write it as a narrative letter to your partner. You can imagine a dialogue and write in what you assume your partner would say, or as a list, sentence fragments, or whatever way you want. Write until you've said it all, until you've gotten it all out of your system. Then, when you are done, put it aside for at least fifteen to thirty minutes. Cool down. Get some water. Let your body relax and allow your emotions to balance again (see Worksheet 7).

5. Step four was to get all that pent up emotion out. Now that it's out there, you've "said" what you've been keeping inside, and you can now start to heal.

Look at your first obstacle and the corresponding emotions. On a new sheet of paper you will start your "I" statement.

Start by writing, "I feel _____." In the blank write your emotion(s) followed by, "when you _____." In this blank write the obstacle.

**Example:** "I feel alone and hurt when you end up getting drunk."

The next two steps are new. You write why and what you want:

**Example:** "I feel (emotion), when you (obstacle), because _____. I want _____."

By writing your "I" statement this way, you are telling your partner how you feel when they do something. You then go on to explain what causes that emotion, followed by what you want to make things better.

Example: "I feel alone and hurt when you end up drunk, because you often yell at me or ignore me. I want you to stop drinking until you are drunk, so we can be happy like we used to be."

Feel free to make appropriate changes to the "I" statement template. The important part of this activity is to express your feelings without attacking your partner. Do this for each obstacle you have listed (see Worksheet 8).

6. Read what you have written in step four once more. This was your say-what-you-need-to-say writing. You don't want to refer to this nor have your partner read it. I tell folks to burn it. Some won't, but many will. By burning this rant, you are releasing it from where it's been hidden. You've got it out in the open. You've used it to create your "I" statement, and by burning it you're releasing those frustrations and moving forward.

7. It's time to come together to read your "I" statements to one another. This process may have taken a few days from when you started in step one. But now you're coming together to be good listeners, not interrupters. It's time to be communicators, not yellers. It's time to accept what each other says, not negate it. It's time to nod, to apologize, to take responsibility, and to put yourselves in each others' shoes. It is not time to attack, blame, threaten, defend, nor name-call.

One partner reads an "I" statement and stops. There's no need for more explanation. The other partner then repeats the "I" statement and stops. Now that both partners have spoken, you can have an open, civil discussion about the topic. Consider using terms like:

- I know you didn't mean to, but . . .
- I'm sorry. I didn't know . . .
- You're right. I didn't understand that . . .
- I'm glad you told me. I'll work on it.
- That's going to be hard, but we can do this together.

You want to end the topic with a goal and a plan.

**Example:** "So, the goal is for me to stop drinking. I'll visit an AA group by Friday."

Then the other partner reads their "I" statement and the process continues. There may be tears and hugs and apologies. But, if there is resistance, anger, yelling, and frustration, you may need to seek out a professional to help you get you out of debt.

8. If you can't work through these issues on your own, look into marriage counseling or couple's therapy. You can ask around for referrals or look in the phone book or online (see Worksheet 12). Some workplaces offer such services for free or inexpensively for their employees. Check your insurance to see if you are covered for counseling.

Hopefully your partner will readily accompany you to your counseling appointments. But even if he or she doesn't, feel free to go alone for advice, guidance and skills you can use to get your relationship back on track.

A word of caution: not all therapists or counselors, no matter how good, fit every couple personality-wise. If you don't feel a connection with the professional, you are not obligated to stick with him or her, and don't abandon the idea altogether. Just find another professional and try again until you find the right one for your relationship.

*Key Points for Investing:*
*Get Rid of Your Debt*

✓ You can't build wealth if you are in debt.

✓ Relationship debt is any negative obstacle that outweighs the positive aspects of your relationship.

✓ Pay off your debt by addressing it.

✓ Don't avoid the issues.

✓ Communicate with your partner.

✓ Use "I" statements.

✓ If you can't rectify the issues, utilize a professional.

## Notes

1. *Savings Fitness: A Guide to Your Money and Your Financial Future*, US Department of Labor, 26.
2. DaveMSW, "Living Together? Put It In Writing," Dare to Dream, http://www.dare-to-dream.us/archives/mental_health_treatment/adult_mh_treatment/couples_counseling/.

— Chapter Four —

# BRING A SACK LUNCH

---

$\mathcal{M}$any people claim they are unable to save any money, much less invest, because they have no cash to play with, nothing to set aside. They only see themselves playing catch-up, so they can't see the possibilities around them. In this chapter, you learn that simplicity and little steps are what lead us to reaching our goals.

My cousin, Shelly, for one, says she can't save or invest. She's in debt and falls behind on her bills. May I draw you a picture of Shelly? She drives a late model BMW. Her nails are impeccable. Her hair is always done at a salon. She wears designer clothes, has a beautiful home, travels out of town regularly to spend time with friends, is a member of a gym, and has had some, ahem . . . surgical upgrades.

She's living a lifestyle she can't afford. Therefore, there's nothing left to invest. If she drove a less expensive car, did her own nails and hair, wore more affordable clothes, traveled less, and bought some weights and exercise DVDs instead of forking over a monthly gym membership fee, I'll bet she'd have a few bucks to stash aside for the future.

That's the point of the sack lunch analogy. A good financial advisor could help you find ways to change your spending habits so you could have something to invest. For example, the advisor might suggest you take a sack lunch to work every day instead of eating out, and while you're at it, forgo the daily Starbucks visits. That will save you $250 a month. If you take that $250 and set it aside in a fund yielding a modest 5 percent, compounded monthly for thirty years, you'd have a quarter of a million dollars. That's 250 thousand dollars for brewing your own Joe and bringing a bologna sandwich to work.

The magic of this method is that you make a small change. You give up just a little, but you do it consistently, and then let time take over the rest. You don't have to get a second job or skip your summer trips to the Grand Tetons. You just make a lunch five days a week.

Little things add up. If you want to save money, invest, and build a strong financial portfolio, your financial advisor will tell you to look at your budget and see where you can start cutting. You need to spend *below* your means in order to have capital to put away for your retirement.

That means you need to be vigilant of every penny you spend. In the world of business, according to Warren Buffett—one of the richest men on the planet, who is worth an estimated $62 billion[1]—it may mean painting only the side of your office building that faces the road. Warren Buffett once acquired a company whose owner counted the sheets in rolls of 500-sheet toilet paper to see if he was being cheated (he was).

You don't have to go that far in personal finance, but for the individual investor it may mean passing on the double latte every morning, trading rounds of golf at the private club for the municipal course, walking ten minutes to the store instead of driving, and cutting your cable choices from 700 to 50 channels.

As your relationship advisor, my advice would be the same. You don't need to do something incredibly grand to have a relationship portfolio that is constantly growing. You don't need to buy your husband a new car, arrange a surprise second wedding for your wife, or put together a weeklong trip to Paris to build your relationship wealth. All you really need are consistent small changes over time.

Like Shelly and her finances, I've heard so many couples complain that they have no time to devote to romance with their partners. Life is busy with work, emails, the kids, and household duties (those are your nails, new cars, trips, and implants). Within all of this, you need to find something to give (your "sack lunch" of the day).

# Finding the Time

No matter what, you and your partner need to squeeze out time for each other during your busy lives. Since there are only twenty-four hours in a day to work with, you've got to give up one-fourth to one-third of those hours to sleep. Probably one-third to one-half of the hours are devoted for work. You've got to eat (bologna sandwich, of course), use the restroom, help the kids with homework, and do the dishes. Life's demands don't leave much time to play. We decide how to use our free time. Do we watch *Dancing with the Stars*, take a nap, check our emails, call a friend, read the newspaper? Or do we devote time to our partner?

We *need* to put in time *every day* to connect with our partners. We need to talk about our days (the good and the bad), tell a joke we heard at work, or relay a topic we heard on talk radio. It doesn't really matter so much what we talk about, as long as we communicate regularly in a healthy way, because when we stop communicating regularly—and I'm not talking about, "Can you get me a pickle while you're up?" or "What time is Corey's game tomorrow?"—we find ourselves drifting apart. When you drift apart long enough, you wake up next to someone you no longer know, and you shouldn't be sleeping with strangers. So you find yourself in either a miserable relationship or a miserable divorce.

The reason we drift is because we change. We change every single day. The man I am today writing these words is not exactly the same man who went to bed last night. I've changed ever so slightly. What we see, hear, do, and experience on a minute-to-minute basis redefines who we are. That's why at high school reunions, although people may say, "You haven't changed a bit," they always end up chatting with their significant other in the car about all the changes they've noticed in their old classmates

(Side note: And what does someone ask his significant other? "Have I changed that much too?"

"Of course not, honey. You haven't changed a bit . . . except your waist size and the flatulence thing, but other than that, not at all.")

When you communicate with someone on a regular basis, those little, daily changes go virtually unnoticed. Your brain processes them subconsciously and rewrites your definition of who you are.

You accept these changes without thinking about them, without even noticing them. But as you grow and change as an individual, you and your spouse are also growing and changing as a couple— either moving in the same direction in tandem because you're connected, or away from each other because you don't communicate. We assimilate our partner's changes as they do ours, and we adjust to these changes, allowing them to fit into our definition of our relationship.

The problem arises when we live together but rarely connect. We pass each other in the kitchen; leave a note on the dining room table; call to ask what to pick up at the Chinese restaurant; but we are no longer communicating. Every day we change without connecting, and we risk moving *away* from our partner instead of moving with them.

If you have enough days of missed connections, you're suddenly living with one of those people from the high school reunion. You remember who the person used to be, but he or she is no longer that person.

Therefore, connecting and communicating daily is integral to building a successful relationship. However, if you think that you don't have the time, what do you do? Change your perception. Shelly has the perception that she doesn't have expendable cash. She needs to change her perception in order to invest. The way you do that in your relationship is to find time in your day. And if you can't find it, make time!

"But I really don't have the time! What am I supposed to do? I have to work. I have to sleep. I have to eat!"

Look at what you do between sleeping, working, and eating. That's where you make your sacrifices. Look, we all make choices. We have a mental list of priorities. We may reason that we need to hit the gym after work to wind down while also staying in shape. Well, if you can't give it up, figure out a way to get your partner to the gym with you. Hop on the stationary bikes for twenty minutes, and talk about your day together. If your relationship is important to you, you absolutely can and will make connecting daily a priority.

Consider talking over dinner. Sit down each night and converse about your day, your dreams, and your future. Gotta take a shower, don't you? Well, shower together. The warm water is soothing. The steam can even be a little sexy. Chat while you scrub his back or rinse her hair.

The reality is that communication is only 10 percent verbal and 30 percent the tone we use when we speak. That leaves a whopping 60 percent of communication based solely on body language.[2] Yes, talk about something that matters, but more important, watch *how* you say it. And, most important, be aware of your body language.

You could tell your partner how much she means to you, but if your tone doesn't match what you're saying, your posture is closed, your eyes don't make contact, and you sit across the room, you could very well have just told her that you're considering sleeping in separate beds.

But if your voice tone is warm or jovial and you laugh and smile, make eye contact, sit close, and even touch her, you could be talking about the day the trash man comes, and it will feel like love.

"But we have kids. They monopolize our dinner chatter, and we can't escape to the shower together while they're up."

Then, wait until they're asleep. Put the kids down and know that the next twenty minutes is your time to connect as a couple. Or go to bed thirty minutes early and chat while you snuggle. And by all means, if you want to find a way to really buy into this sack lunch idea, turn off the TV and keep clear of the computer. For the really adventurous, consider experimenting with a "no TV or no computer" day once a week or so. I bet you'll have plenty of time to reconnect on those days.

I saw a survey in a parenting magazine not too long ago. Sixteen hundred moms were asked, "If you had one hour to yourself before bedtime, what would you do?" And 59 percent of moms chose to "read, watch TV, or go online." Only one out of ten said they'd make love to their husbands.

So for goodness sake, people! It's time to unplug the plasma and laptops and get back to connecting with one another.

## Carl the Gas Station Guy

I go to the same gas station every week. I know the owner, Carl. Carl works six or seven days a week, maybe ten to twelve hours each day.

He's a nice guy with a wife and a fourteen-year-old daughter. When I pay for my gas or buy lottery scratcher tickets for my grandmother, sometimes I'll spend a few extra minutes to chat with Carl.

After going to his gas station for over four years, one day we talked about the weather, the Lakers, nothing too heavy. Then I asked him, "How's the wife and kid?"

"Fine, I guess," he said. "I mean, my daughter's doing great in school, but I work so much that when I come home, I try to spend time with her before she goes to sleep. But then I'm too pooped to do anything else. So I plop down and watch TV. In other words, I don't really get much time with my wife."

"Well, what's she doing while you're watching TV?"

"I don't know," Carl admitted. "She's busy."

"Carl, turn off the TV and plop her down next to you. Ask her about her day and tell her about yours."

"She doesn't want to hear about my day."

"Give it a try."

I come back the following week, and I ask him what happened.

"See, I told you. She didn't want to hear about my day."

"Why? What happened?"

"She said she was too busy to talk."

"What was she doing?"

"Making mine and my daughter's lunches for the next day and washing dishes from dinner."

I told Carl that it didn't mean she didn't want to hear about his day; she probably felt like there was too much to do to sit on the couch. I told him to get off the couch, wash the dishes as she made the lunches, and ask her about her day. Carl balked and hesitated, but said he'd give it a shot.

Next time I saw him, Carl was wearing a huge grin.

"It worked. We talked. And she really wanted to hear about my day. And we laughed. We actually laughed. We haven't laughed together in a long time."

Carl and his wife now have a daily routine. She makes the lunches, and he does the dinner dishes each night. Then they retire to the couch and continue their conversation as they cuddle or exchange hand and foot rubs. Carl says he's a much happier man, and his relationship with his wife is ten times stronger than it used to be.

Be careful not to neglect your relationship portfolio. When you neglect it, you stop investing; your capital either flatlines, or you find yourself losing ground, something you *never* want to happen in your relationship. Maybe you come home late now and then. You may leave the dirty dishes for your partner. You have "Ladies Night Out" with your girlfriends every Saturday. And in the process, your communication is dwindling. These are all small "expenses," and they're bound to happen now and again. And to be honest, that's okay, just as buying that latte every so often is fine. But if you find yourself guilty of too many relationship "expenses," you're going to find yourself depleting the portfolio you've worked so hard to build.

Just a little sacrifice is all it takes. The beauty of bringing the sandwich to work is that after awhile, it no longer feels like a sacrifice. It becomes a way of life. You get used to it. And when you do, you can build upon it with another small sacrifice, like stashing 50 dollars a month from your paycheck into a CD. In your relationship, this could mean making sure you hold hands every day or kiss good night before you turn in. When you allow these little efforts to grow consistently, they build upon themselves—just like compound interest—adding more strength, depth, and volume (like a good shampoo) to your relationship portfolio. When you consistently invest your efforts, your relationship wealth grows quickly. Let those efforts—that time together and daily connections—compound, and in thirty years you'll have a relationship portfolio strong, rich, and full of love, something you can sit back and marvel at proudly.

## Portfolio-Stretching Exercise

Try this for a week. If you and your partner enjoy it and find it useful, continue with the exercise for as long as you both want.

1. First, both of you get one of those little note pads, the kind you can stick in your pocket or purse. Then stick it in your pocket

or purse (well, what did you expect?), and be sure you have a pen with you.

2. For the next week, whenever you two are apart and you think of something you would have said to your partner if you were together, mentioned to them, or commented on, jot it down. You don't need to write a book here; just a sentence or a few key words to help you recall the topic later on.

3. You can do this at work, at home, or in the car. I am big on the car thing. In my car I've always kept a few pens and scraps of paper to jot things down, so I can bring them up with my wife when I get home. Two reasons the car works for me: 1) The music and the DJs' banter between songs reminds me of things I want to say to my wife; 2) When I turn the radio off, I do some of my best thinking (my other best thinking times are just before I fall asleep and when I shower). But writing notes and driving is not exactly safe. I recently found an incredibly easy to use, small, powerful, and inexpensive voice recorder called Word Up, available at www.sms3insb.com/wordup.htm. Instead of the pad, now I take my Word Up with me wherever I go, and I leave little messages to myself.

4. No matter if you jot them down or record the ideas, when you get home, make it a point to cover all of the topics you and your partner saved during the day. It doesn't matter so much when you do it, but you both need to squeeze out the time to talk together. Do you need to sit face-to-face on the sofa? No, but you do need to avoid other major distractions. You can pull a "Carl, the Gas Guy" and share chores together while you chat. You can jog or bike, or use some of the other ideas offered in this chapter—in the shower, at dinner, or after the kids are in bed. But be sure distractions like email and the TV are eliminated.

Hopefully you'll find connecting daily will not be an inconvenience but become a way of life. It can bring you and your partner closer each day, compounding the investment connections you have made previously, while building your relationship wealth gradually and consistently.

## *Key Points for Investing:*
## *Bring a Sack Lunch*

✓ Make small sacrifices consistently.

✓ Communicate with your partner daily.

✓ Invest in your relationship, or you'll end up drifting apart.

✓ We all change, but it's best to change *together*.

✓ Find, or make, time to connect regularly.

**Notes**

1. Warren Buffett, "10 Ways to Get Rich," *Parade Magazine*, Sept. 7, 2008, 5.
2. Judy H. Wright, *The Power of Using Encouraging Words and the Law of Attraction* (Missoula, MT: Artichoke Press, 2006).

# Chapter Five

# INVEST REGULARLY AND DIVERSIFY

For normal folks, investing regularly and consistently is the key to making their money grow. Ask any financial advisor; it's simple to save a little here and a little there when things are going smoothly in your financial world. You've gotten a recent raise, just paid off your car, and the credit card bill is finally at a zero balance. At moments like these, you have a few extra bucks, and you're feeling good.

But what happens when you take a pay cut at work, get a surprise medical bill, or have to start paying for childcare? Not so carefree with the moolah any more, are you? You feel a need to tighten your belt in order to make ends meet. Often we put saving and investing on the back burner because investing is all about the future, while today we're worried about the here and now.

But what's that? Do you hear it? It's the faint voice of your financial advisor. And what's he telling you? "Stick a little aside anyway. Figure out a way to continue investing, even if it's just a little."

This is what's happening right now in our country. Folks are losing their jobs, losing their investments, and losing their homes. Many are in survival mode. Should they still continue to save and invest? Yes. It could be as little as twenty bucks a month into a money market account or fifty dollars into a fixed annuity IRA. Even in a bear market, there are safe places to put your money, allowing it to grow for the future.

The same holds true for relationships. We need to invest regularly and consistently in our relationship portfolio, good times or bad. It's pretty easy to invest during the good times: work is great, the kids are doing well in school, you've been hitting the gym regularly, and vacation is two weeks away. When you feel good about yourself and your life, it's easy to see the good in your relationship, and when you see that, you invest in it. You communicate more, flirt more, make love more, help your partner more often, offer more compliments, and joke around and smile with them more frequently.

But when the market is low, when life is tough, it's difficult to see the romance-forest for the trees. Bills are piling up, you've had the flu for a week, your new boss is a tyrant, and your dog bit the mailman. Your mind is preoccupied, so you end up putting the relationship lower on your life's priority list. Yet, these times, more than any other, are when you need to invest the most. When you invest during the tough stints, the benefits are not only long-term but are also immediate, helping your tough time become easier. It's like non-taxed contributions we can make now and how we build tax-deferred interest we can use later. As long as we are being consistent, investing regularly, even when we don't initially feel like it, we will build that portfolio.

The funny thing is, if you understand the universal law of attraction, which tells us that we become what we believe and what we do, investing when you are having a hard time is *exactly* what's needed at that time. When we feel strapped financially, we scrimp and worry over every penny. Makes sense, right? But, as a result, we're virtually announcing to the entire universe, "We don't have enough!" The universe responds with, "Okay," and we find ourselves in a continuous downward financial spiral.

The universe also responds this way to relationships. When we see all the bad and focus on the negative, it's easier to find more to gripe about. Conversely, the moment we start focusing on the positive, when we start putting romance back into our relationships, when we go back to our romantic investments, the relationship grows and prospers and becomes positive again.

Dean Karlan, an economist at Yale University, discovered that in some underdeveloped countries like the Philippines, if low-income individuals were reminded to save some of their income, many would.[1] Richard Thaler, a behavior economist and professor at the University of Chicago says that the only real way to save is to have an automatic deduction pulled from your paycheck regularly.[2] What we need are reminders and ways to invest automatically. We'll discuss these "tricks" for our relationship in the next chapter.

## Diversification

You also need to diversify. The financial investor should be spreading his investments among different sectors and products: real estate, stocks, mutual funds, CDs, money market accounts, tax-sheltered annuities, 401Ks, IRAs, and so on. Where the individual is in life (career, age, family), as well as what the market is dictating, will determine which ones to go heavier in and which ones to go lighter.

Like the financial investor, the relationship investor has many products to choose from: dates, flirtation, public displays of affection, cuddling, sexual intimacy, little surprises, small gifts, big gifts, love notes, romantic adventures, trips . . . the list is endless. You choose your product based on finances, time, resources, mood, children, work, and many other factors. Again, it's important to diversify and change things up, so all your proverbial relationship eggs are not in one basket, no matter how sturdy it may appear.

## Daily, Monthly, Annually

Diversification also includes looking at how you invest. The savvy financial investor is making calculated moves daily: shopping during sales, using coupons at the grocery store, and putting the savings in their bank account. They're working monthly, utilizing paycheck dividends to stash in their 401Ks and TSAs, as well as having their bills and mutual funds paid through automatic withdrawals. There's also a good chance they're making use of annual saving, maybe taking any windfalls (a yearly bonus at work or a federal tax refund) and opening a new CD or buying some shares of Intel Corporation.

Relationships have their own daily, monthly, and annual investments as well. Your daily savings are holding hands, saying, "I love you," hugging, kissing, and snuggling. These are your coupons and sale shopping. They may not seem much, but a little bit every day ends up being a great long-term investment.

Monthly, go on dates. Like the automatic withdrawals and paycheck deductions, regular dates each month are your bread and butter in the relationship investment world. I'll get more into dates in the next chapter.

Your annual event is usually a biggie, something you can't do very often that may take a lot of prep time. Like a tax refund, you could pull it off once a year. These usually boost your portfolio in one fell swoop (what the heck does that mean anyway? Is that alluding to a bird dive or something?). Whereas daily investments add a little each day for slow growth, the annual investment will probably add just about as much as a year of daily investing. These are the Romantic Adventures we'll be exploring in chapter six.

If you incorporate daily, monthly, and yearly relationship investing into your life and stick with them, your connection and love for your partner is guaranteed to grow.

## New Sectors

Finally, try to expand your investing by going out of your comfort zone. Invest in areas you are familiar with, but also try something new now and again. Start off small, and if you see a return, add more weight into this sector. If you get no return, you still have your biggest investments in the areas you're most familiar with, and you can try investing outside of the box with another product.

For instance, feel free to go to the same restaurant you always go to, get her favorite flowers, or buy him his favorite magazine. But you can also try mixing things up a bit: a new restaurant, a different bouquet of flowers, a book you think he may enjoy, signing up for a cooking class, a new position from the *Kama Sutra* . . . whatever you're in the mood for. The worst that can happen is you don't like it. The best? You have another weapon in your investment arsenal.

My wife had been bugging (I mean asking) me to take a swing dance class with her for years. I was reluctant, not because I can't dance; I can. I'm a very good dancer. I look forward to going to weddings just for the dancing at the reception (dancing, and those candy-coated almonds that they always put on your table right before you eat). But I wasn't excited having someone tell me what count I should be on and where my left foot should be in front of a bunch of I-can't-swing-dance-either strangers. So, you know what I did? No, I didn't join a class with my wife. I bought us (read, "her") a "How to Swing Dance" DVD. This appeased her for a few weeks, until she realized it was collecting dust.

So my wonderful wife, Mary, asked me when we're going to use it. I saw no harm, so we opened the package, popped it in the machine, and started lesson number one: rock forward, rock back, step, step. We progressed through the different levels, dancing in front of the TV to Benny Goodman tunes about twice a week.

About three months later, Mary told me she still wanted us to take a swing class. I guess me spinning her around the living room as I wore a pair of boxers, a Homer Simpson T-shirt, and a pair of white socks was not her idea of romance.

Apparently, all that DVD practice just added to her desire to take the class. She felt she had enough of the basics to walk in to a class of strangers and not have two left feet. There was nothing else for me to do but to do it. We signed up, got a regular babysitter for an hour every Wednesday for eight weeks, and next thing we knew, we were at a local community center with a bunch of other couples (some of the fellas looked like they'd also lost the let's-just-buy-the-DVD battle), triple-stepping and rock-stepping our way through Basic Swing 101.

After every lesson, Mary and I would share an ice cream, laugh at ourselves, and make up histories about the other couples at the community center. To be honest, I never really got into the dancing, but I did look forward to our regular Wednesday mini-outings each week. After two months of swing-outs and hand-switches, both Mary and I had had our fair share of West Coast Swing and retired our Arthur Murray shoes for good.

We had stepped out of our comfort zones (I actually fell out of mine) and tried a new investment product. Although it had been eye opening and the after dancing investment was great, it wasn't what we were looking for. So we moved on to new products. That's the beauty of not putting all your eggs in one basket. You can always pull out and move on, as long as you keep diversifying and investing consistently and regularly.

It's important to realize that no matter what you invest in, new products or the old stand-bys, sometimes you just won't show gains.

At times, you may invest, diversify, and change up the sectors, but your portfolio flat-lines or maybe even loses a bit. Do *not* stop investing in your relationship. It happens in finance and it happens in romance. Sometimes there's a bear market, and sometimes there's a bull. But you plug away, because as long as there's nothing fundamentally wrong with the relationship, your portfolio will bounce back—guaranteed! Your relationship could be affected by stress at work, a deadline, concern for a friend or family member, sickness, and several other issues. When our minds are preoccupied, our relationships will often lose a step, but as long as we keep investing, they'll eventually take two more steps forward.

## Portfolio-Stretching Exercise

1. Sit down with your partner and make a list of ways you can invest. Anything you can think of qualifies—the simple to the complex; the easy and the nearly impossible; things you've done, are doing, want to do, and might consider trying.

   Feel free to list touches (hugs, snuggles, hand holds, specific body part massages), activities (going to the beach, camping, dancing, gardening), sexual ideas (new positions, toys, locations, role playing), trips (Vegas, a bed and breakfast, the Bahamas, Disney World), and anything else, *including* things you haven't tried and would think might add to your portfolio if you share them with your partner.

2. Neither of you are allowed to shoot down any responses from your partner; no grimaces, groans, or glares—just acceptance. Just brainstorm and let the ideas flow, and one idea will probably lead to the next three. Keep this up until you have exhausted your idea bank or until the 11:00 news comes on.

3. Now if *you* made a suggestion, but no longer think it was a good idea, you can ask your partner if she thinks it should be eliminated from the list. If she agrees with you, scratch it. If she

wants it on the list, keep it. (See! Never should've mentioned clam digging, should you?) The only ideas that can be removed are the ones brought up by the partner who initiated them. If your partner posted an idea and it's not working for you, if he doesn't suggest its removal, you must let it be.

4. List the ideas that remain on three separate sheets of paper labeled "Daily," "Monthly," and "Annually."

   The investments and deposits that you both think can be done on a daily, or near-daily, basis will be listed on your "Daily" page. Ideas like "Say 'I love you,'" "kiss," or "share a fifteen minute talk."

   The ideas you can do every few weeks, months, or bimonthly will be listed on the "Monthly" page: going to Luigi's for dinner, or staying at a bed and breakfast.

   The "Annually" page will be the biggies, like an Alaskan cruise or running a marathon together.

   You may find that you'll want to put an idea under two categories. Do whatever works for your relationship. Remember, nothing's written in blood (unless, of course, you're into that sort of thing) and I'm not going to knock on your door to see your lists. This is for the benefit of your relationship, so make it work for you.

5. Highlight any of the items on the three pages that you both haven't shared yet. These are your new products, your untouched sectors. If one of you has done something but the other has not, it is considered "new" for this exercise.

6. Post your three pages where both of you see them easily (alongside the bathroom mirror, on the fridge, on the ceiling over your bed) and start investing regularly.

   Try implementing your daily deposits and savings right away. Look at the areas that you feel comfortable with and get to it. You don't have to do everything, but if you are feeling adventurous, maybe try one of the ideas you questioned. And feel free to discuss these ideas as a team.

For the "Monthly" list, start looking at some ideas you think would be fun to implement in the next month or so. Talk about what you both would enjoy and figure out a way to schedule it into your calendar. The next chapter will offer more details regarding this.

As for the "Annually" page, you can work on this as a couple or plan a surprise for your partner. You'll probably need to look far in advance for preparations and start working on it a few months ahead of time. For specific annual ideas and romantic adventures, read chapter six.

7. Every month or so, be sure to look over your highlighted ideas and choose one you'll try as a couple. (It would be good to choose a specific day like the first of each month). If it works for you both, implement it into your regular deposits. If not, toss it, and the next month try another.

### *Key Points for Investing: Invest Regularly and Diversify*

- ✓ Investing regularly and consistently is the key to making your portfolio grow.
- ✓ Investing is easy in good times.
- ✓ It's harder in tough times, but still worthwhile.
- ✓ Diversify your romance investments into different sectors.
- ✓ Invest daily, monthly, and annually.
- ✓ Try something new every now and then.

**Notes**
1. Tim Harford, "How to Save Smarter," *Parade Magazine*, May 10, 2009, 10.
2. Ibid.

— CHAPTER SIX —

# KEEP IT PAINLESS

---

To invest, or save money, all you have to do is not to spend—right? Wrong. "Not spending" is static and inactive. When you save, that's a choice. It's active. You are doing! Who would have thought that saving would be such a tough chore? When the Average Joe first starts saving, he often wonders, "Where the heck am I going to find some extra dough to put away?"

The best place to begin is with a budget. To design a budget that works for you, start by recording all of your expenses for a month: groceries, wardrobe, gasoline, restaurant visits, cigarettes, lattes, everything. Next, look at how much money you're bringing home each month. If your expenses outweigh your income (simple third grade math here), you're digging a hole your financial advisor calls debt (by the way, everyone else calls it debt too).

If you are in debt, that means you owe. If you owe, by definition, you not only have nothing to invest, but you also need to give the next dollar you earn to the bill collector.

A budget is helpful because it allows you to see where you're spending and over-spending. It gives you the opportunity to trim the fat, cut back on the smokes and lattes, dig yourself out of that debt-hole, and help you ascend the foothills of investment. Trimming the fat can be a hard pill to swallow at first, because you may have to change your lifestyle (see Chapter 4: "Bring A Sack Lunch"):

fewer dinners out, shopping for clothes when there's a sale, and only buying gold-plated mouth grills versus the 24-karat good stuff you used to wear.

What you need to do is live at a lower economic level than your salary reflects. By spending less than you earn and having your investments automatically withdrawn from your check each month, investing starts to feel painless. You may not even notice your lifestyle shift, because it becomes a lifestyle instead of a shift.

Your job is to make regular deposits. Remember from the last chapter: you don't try to outthink the trends. You just keep plugging away with your consistent monthly investments in your TSA, ROTH IRA, mutual funds, and eventually your investing becomes a way of life. It becomes habitual. You no longer think of it as an inconvenience, just as you don't think of brushing your teeth every morning as an inconvenience. It's part of your daily routine . . . isn't it?

In the same way, you can make romance a lifestyle. When you build your relationship portfolio you don't avoid the inevitable ripples. Avoiding ripples, like saving, is inactive. Building your relationship portfolio, like investing, is dynamic. There's thought, work, and action involved. So when you *communicate* concerning the ripples between you and your partner, you are actively building your relationship portfolio.

## Finding the Time

Where do you find the extra time and energy to invest in your relationship? You need to make a budget. What does a relationship budget look like? Consider how you spend your time during a typical week and write it down: work, sleep, eating, watching TV, homework with the kids, talking on the phone, checking emails, reading the paper, going shopping, showering, watering the garden, surfing the web—everything. Write it all down.

Now, where can you trim the fat to allow for a date or two a month? You may have to force the kids to water the garden, or TiVo an episode of *CSI*, or—heaven forbid!—cut back on the web surfing. Next, sit down with your partner and a calendar, and schedule your romance.

In finance, "A budget is how you know how much you have to

work with and where your money's going," says Dave Ramsey, the author of the bestselling *The Total Money Makeover*. "And make sure you and your spouse agree on it. If you're not working together, it's almost impossible to win with money. If you both create the plan, you'll be prepared no matter what situation comes your way."[1]

"Awwww," you say, "where's the spontaneity in that?"

Screw spontaneity! If you are not connecting romantically on a regular basis, schedule it. Schedule date nights. Schedule getaways. Schedule sex, for goodness sake! Sure, you can be spontaneous in addition to this scheduling. No one's taking that away from you. And if you actually follow through with what you slap on the calendar, you'll be more apt to be a bit more impromptu. But let's start with your budget first.

Mary Hunt, a regular financial contributor for *Woman's Day Magazine* and the force behind the website DebtProofLiving.com recommends folks pay themselves first.[2] Before buying anything else, stash 10 percent of your income into savings and investments. Well, if it's good enough for Hunt, it's good enough for building a relationship portfolio.

At the first of the month, before you schedule meetings and hitting the gym, pay yourself first. Pencil in your dates. Get together with your partner on the first day of the month and look at planners, Blackberries, and the kids' calendars and schedules, then pencil in your romance before all else. When other events come up, they'll have to fit around your relationship. That gives your relationship first place on your priority list.

## Make It a Habit

If you make scheduling a habit ("Oh, it's the first of the month; get out your calendar."), investing in your relationship portfolio becomes painless and second nature, like brushing your teeth.

Let me tell you a story about yours truly. When I first started dating my wife, I planned romantic adventures for her each year. It was my annual "windfall" (see last chapter). It took work, creativity, and planning.

A romantic adventure is one of those annual windfalls you deposit into your account once a year or so. Mary Zalmanek wrote an incredible book called *The Art of the Spark* to inspire couples to attempt and follow through on romantic adventures. These adventures take planning, time, and preparation and are generally remembered for a lifetime. At the end of this chapter, I want to share with you a romantic adventure shared between Erinn and Becca, but first let me tell you one that I created.

One year, a couple days before her birthday, I called my wife's boss and told him that my wife, Mary, needed the next three days off, but she didn't know it yet. I told him my plan, and he agreed to free her from her obligations at work.

At the time Mary and I shared a car. After I picked her up from work, she asked, "Where are we going, Leon? This isn't the way home." I just smiled and drove on, virtually kidnapping my partner. (By the way, actual kidnapping is a crime; virtual kidnapping is questionable . . . do not really kidnap your partner!)

After forty minutes her curiosity was piqued, especially since home was only five minutes away. To distract her I'd brought a duffle bag with two different outfits in it, and I asked her to change, killing fifteen more minutes. At the time, I was a front desk manager at a beautiful all-suites property in Southern California. As we approached Pismo Beach, I told Mary that I needed to drop off some brochures at a sister hotel before we continued our journey. When I returned, I said, "You have to see this room, Mary. It's incredible."

She accompanied me to a room with a patio overlooking the Pacific Ocean. There was a fireplace in the sitting room, balloons, a "Happy Birthday" banner, rose petals on the canopy bed and in the bathtub, a bottle of chilled champagne, and a massage kit with oils and powders.

Mary looked around in awe. "Are you sure we should be in here? It looks like someone is preparing for a big surprise," she said.

Of course the surprise was for her. I'd packed too many clothes, brought her entire cosmetic drawer, every hair product I could find, and enough cash to cover anything I'd forgotten.

It was a terribly romantic and memorable adventure, one that she will never forget. And one of many that I used.

Then, of course, the inevitable occurred. With so many romantic adventures, we were bound to have a child sooner or later. Becoming a parent, I found my time and energy zapped with diaper changes, middle of the night feedings, and milestones. I found I just didn't have the time or energy to devote to romantic adventures. A few years later, Baby Number Two arrived (beats me how this one occurred with the lack of romantic adventures in our lives). I found myself using being a father as an excuse for not being as romantic as I had once been.

Once you have a significant interruption in your routine, it can be hard to get back on track again. You've got to go through the process all over: making a promise to yourself, finding ways to cut back, and feeling uncomfortable again.

Seven years after Baby Number One popped her head into the world—we still call our daughters "Baby Number One" and "Baby Number Two"; it makes things easier, and there was no arguing over names for me and Mary—I decided to recommit to making romance a lifestyle again, therefore making it painless. I created the "52-Week Challenge."

## The Challenge

I love challenges. I don't care what it is. If it's a challenge, I'm there. If you call it a competition or a contest, I may be interested. But use the word *challenge*, and I must accept, which is why I called it the "52-Week Challenge." The premise was simple: do something romantic for my wife once a week for fifty-two weeks. The catch was I couldn't repeat anything from prior weeks. I mean, I could, but it wouldn't count. (If you can do something consistently for a year, it becomes a habit and a lifestyle, natural and quite painless too!)

I compiled a list of ideas from books, friends, the Internet, episodes of *Sponge Bob Square Pants*, and the like. It was easy. I chose all the simple ideas first: write a love letter, clean her car, surprise her by bringing home a dessert.

By week twelve all the easy ones were gone and things became a little strained. Not only did I have to invest more effort and creativity, but the novelty of a different romantic idea each week started to wear a little thin. But I knew all too well that this happened whenever someone made a New Year's Resolution. (Going to the gym is great. That sore feeling and waking up at 6:00 a.m. makes you feel alive until about March when it starts making you feel dead. You throw in the towel, and you're back to being the blob you were the year before.)

I had to ride the crest of this wave of doubt because the other side promised a glorious view.

By week twenty-five, I got my groove back. And by week forty, romance was becoming habitual for me again. Sometimes I didn't even need the list. It was no longer a chore. It was as natural as cleaning socks. Besides, my wife loved it, and our relationship flourished.

By the end of the year, romance was back in our lives as a lifestyle—easy, routine, and painless—and it still is today.

## Create a Budget

Okay, what can you do to make romance painless? Plan it like a budget. Sit down and plan to get the heck away—not from each other, but from the stresses of everyday life. A survey of American Counselors and Therapists asked what one thing they thought could save a struggling marriage. Eighty percent of the respondents answered, "Regular weekends away." That's time alone . . . together!

Could it benefit couples that aren't struggling? You bet your sweet peaches it can. It's always better to be proactive than reactive! So start getting away together. Weekends are ideal, but not always realistic. In addition to getaways, plan and have regular dates. Make them commonplace, routine, and painless.

How often should you and your partner date? Monthly? Bimonthly? Weekly? If you can go weekly, great, but it's better to ease into something like this, like a hot bath. Step in. Get accustomed to the temperature. Then when it feels right, slowly lower yourself. Continue easing yourself in until you're leaving a nice ring around the tub.

I would shoot for once a month to start with. That's only twelve dates a year. We can all handle that. Think of these dates as the monthly deposits mentioned in the previous chapter. When one date a month feels comfortable, try two a month.

My wife and I started to invest for the first time soon after getting married. We scrimped to come up with twenty-five bucks a month. We looked for possible savings anywhere we could. I remember we would save something like thirty cents a week buying the medium size eggs at the grocery store versus the large. It was tough at first, but we grew accustomed to it. When we were comfortable, we stretched ourselves to fifty dollars a month. Then one hundred dollars a month. It was a gradual process over the years, but now we invest a sizable portion of our income monthly, and we don't even notice because we have stretched ourselves gradually over time.

If you asked me to do the splits right now, I would tear something more than just my pants, but with gradual training and stretching myself a little each day . . . well, I'd probably still tear something, but you get the idea.

To keep yourself honest, pencil these investments (dates) into your planners. Post them on your calendars. Program them into your Blackberries. I love the site, MemoToMe.com. It's a free site that reminds you of whatever dates you need help remembering. It's like your own personal Ginko Biloba tree online.

You plug in your date and tell the site when to remind you about it. Then you go about your life until you get your email about the Spice Girls Revival band concert on Friday night.

According to Jan Dahlin Geiger, CFP, MBA, a budget, or spending plan "is a road map to lead you away from debt and toward saving money."[3] Penciling in dates is your road map in leading you away from a stagnant relationship toward passion and excitement.

The reason it's so important to write these dates on calendars and punch them into PDAs is purely psychological. When we write something down and refer to it later, we're more apt to follow through with it. Lee Iacocca said, "The discipline of writing something down is the first step toward making it happen."[4] Seventy percent of people do *not* write down their New Year's resolutions, and simply lose track of them.

The other reason to write down your "specific date night" or pop it into your online calendar is also psychological; it gives you something to look forward to. Anticipation often elicits more feel-good chemicals than the actual event itself. Think of waiting for Christmas or a big vacation when you were a kid.

Knowing that you have a date coming up can make the tougher parts of life easier to handle (if, of course, you're excited for the plans and the person who will be with you). The dog peed on your shoes. Someone at work ate your burrito. Some freak keeps calling your home phone and hanging up. But on Saturday, you're going miniature golfing and rock climbing. Everything's going to be *just* fine.

If you have kids, let them see the calendar so they're aware of your date nights. If this is a new component in your family dynamics, you will undoubtedly experience some resistance from the little ones, but just like it will for you, as you make this a regular routine, it will become painless for them too.

## Now What?

I can already hear you say it: "Thank you, oh great and powerful relationship advisor, for telling us to schedule and pencil in monthly dates. But, oh, Wise One, what do we actually pencil in? What do we actually do?"

Great question, and thanks for addressing me with such respect. There are pounds—I mean, *tons*—of literature on the subject. You can read books and pull up websites with lists of ideas for dates—on a budget, special occasions, make an impact, creative dates. Just let your fingers do the walking. If you don't have a computer at your disposal, just flip to chapter ten where I've added a couple more ounces to the tons of literature out there.

For instance, send the kids to Grandma's and rent a DVD. Go out to dinner and a concert. Take a hike and eat a picnic on a summit or the nearest park. The best thing, however, is to play hooky.

Call in sick to work now and then, the both of you. It's a little dangerous, which pumps the adrenaline and creates more sexual chemistry between the two of you. You've got the whole house to yourself—in the middle of that day, no less. The neighbors are gone, kids are at school. Stay in bed until noon. Make love in the garage. Watch *Judge Judy* while you feed each other cupcakes. Be a little decadent. Sometimes naughty can be *nice*.

Do something new and exotic together now and again. That's the "new product investment." Get a gym membership and go together. Plant a bromeliad garden (pineapple family). Go surfing. Take a cooking class. Experiencing something new on a date can be invigorating and draw the two of you closer because you'll both be out of your comfort zones. But you cling to what you know—or maybe you don't really know—your partner!

Now schedule a get-away, and this time really mean it. Give your partner time away from the household responsibilities once in awhile. I know that's technically not a date because you're not together, but it reignites the relationship. Let your partner go on a hike, play a sport, hang with friends, go to the spa, or simply read a book (hopefully this one). Your partner will return happy, energized, fresh, appreciative, and filled with more romantic feelings. But the deal is partners must reciprocate the offer. Soon after, the other one should have the same opportunity. If this becomes a one-sided event, not only will one partner become resentful, but I will also personally come to your home and put glue in your toothpaste tube (and, yes, I will warn your partner first).

### "I'm Yours"

Here's the romantic adventure I promised you. Becca and Erinn had been dating for about ten months. Both in their early twenties, the couple met in college. Becca had a crush on Erinn her first year in school. Soon they were dating, and Erinn wanted to do something special for Becca's birthday. He gave himself a few weeks and started to work on one of the most impressive pieces I have seen displayed on YouTube.

Erinn knew that Becca liked the song, "I'm Yours" by Jason Mraz. Erinn fancied himself as a singer, being a musical theater major and having sung in choirs. The young man also had an interest in film editing.

While Becca headed to Disney World during spring break, Erinn got to work. He searched for clips on YouTube that he needed to make his "band." Then he videotaped himself singing the Jason Mraz song. With different levels of facial stubble, he also sang his own background three times over in order to create the perfect harmony with himself. What he ended up with was himself singing "I'm Yours" with a band he created online from across the globe.

Erinn says that when Becca returned from the Magic Kingdom, he was praying that she would like his birthday gift to her. She surely did. Becca said, "I just love Erinn's voice and at the end of the song, I just lost it," crying tears of joy.

The two are currently in a long-distance relationship, and Becca says that Erinn's Romantic Adventure "gave me confidence in our relationship because he put so much time into it. This may have a real shot at working out."

Check out the video on YouTube. Just punch in "I'm Yours—Erinn's YouTube Band Cover." Becca appreciated the end result, and she thinks it will positively affect her relationship because of the time and effort Erinn was willing to invest on her.

Erinn's example is another way to keep yourself debt-free.

The simplest way to get on the path of wealth is to stay clear of debt and save consistently. The quickest way to get on the path of a happy, romantic relationship is to stay clear of relationship debt (the marital issues we mentioned in chapter three) and save consistently as mentioned in chapter five. That means budget your time and make dates a priority. Your relationship will remain fresh, loving, romantic, and alive.

## Portfolio-Stretching Exercise

1. This should be a fun and rather simple exercise. On the first day of the month, sit with your partner and your planners, PDAs, or family calendar.

2. Look at the engagements you've already planned: the BBQ at the Jorgensons', Tyler's soccer game, taking the old jalopy in for maintenance. From the open days that remain, pencil in dates, home activities, getaways, or romantic adventures. Schedule at least one for the month. If you can do more, even better.

3. While you're at it, compile a list of date ideas: a hike, day at the beach, picnic at the park, lunch and movies, dinner and dancing—whatever. The list needs to have date ideas that both of your agree on.

4. Both of you sign up with MemotoMe.com for free and have the service start reminding you of all of the dates you make each month.

5  For the first one, maybe you can choose the date. Pick one from the list or come up with one of your own. Share it with her or keep it a surprise. If it's a surprise, you'll need to tell her the calendar date, how long the date is expected to last, what to wear, and what to bring (if anything). You'll need to prep her without giving away the surprise.

6. The next month is her turn. And the third month, you two can work together to come up with a date idea on your own or use one from the list.

7. Month four, start all over again. By paying yourselves first, investing in your relationship becomes painless.

⌒⌒⌒

## *Key Points for Investing:*
## *Keep It Painless*

✓ Create a "budget."

✓ Pay yourself first.

✓ Pencil in dates.

✓ Play hooky.

✓ Plan something new.

✓ Get away from one another.

### Notes

1.  Mary Hunt, "The Best Money Advice You'll Ever Get," *Woman's Day Magazine*, February 17, 2010, 106.

2.  Mary Hunt, "7 Big Money Mistakes to Avoid," *Woman's Day Magazine* November 17, 2009, 154.

3.  Jan Dahlin Geiger, *Get Your Assets In Gear* (Outskirts Press, 2007), 52.

4.  "Lee Iacocca Qutoes," Brainy Quote, http://www.brainyquote.com/quotes /quotes/l/leeiacocca149249.html.

— Chapter Seven —

# ASSESS THE RISKS

---

When you're young and just starting to invest, your financial advisor will tell you it's okay to take more risks because you won't need the money for quite some time. The bigger the financial risk, the greater the chance for a larger return. But because it is a risk, there's also a greater chance of losing your investment. That's why time is a huge factor when it comes to risk. The stock market, for instance, has proven, over time—even during times of deep loss—that the investor still makes gains by staying in the market long enough.

If you invested in the market right before the fall of 1929 you'd have had to wait more than twenty years for the market to return to the same level.[1] Funny thing is many investors do just the opposite. They are trying to set themselves up for retirement thirty years away, and they're putting their cash aside in Treasury bonds, fearing the stock market will drop out from under them.[2] So they've guaranteed themselves a return, but one that can barely keep up with inflation, much less sustaining a growing financial portfolio. A risky investment early on in life is more appropriate for the young investor.

As we age and near retirement, we know that we'll need those investments to sustain our lives. We need to be a little less risky and ease up a bit. This "risk adverse" mentality should continue as we get closer to retirement, putting our investments in more conservative products.

Sure, there's less chance of hitting huge returns, but we're also avoiding big losses that could undercut our golden years' cash flow.

So I'm going to tell you to take more risks at the beginning of your relationship, right? And be more conservative as you approach the AARP years, correct? On the contrary! This is the one and only exception to my follow-the-financial-advice-for-your-relationship rule. In this case, you want to do just the opposite . . . well, kind of.

In finance they say take your risks early and gradually become more conservative as you grow older. In relationships we already take the risks early on. No one needs to tell us. It's natural. Brain chemistry dictates this. As we age the chemicals dwindle and we no longer take risks (kind of like finances, right?). However, as your relationship advisor, I'm telling you to go against this natural tendency to leave risk behind, and make a conscious effort to seek risk in your relationship, especially as you grow old together.

Why do we take more risks when we're first in a relationship? It's all Mother Nature's fault. During the beginning stages of a new relationship, Mother Nature, like any good mom, wants to give us a fighting chance to make our relationship a success. She quite literally dopes us up with chemicals and hormones that create an "addiction" for our partners.

These first six to eighteen months of a relationship—when there's excitement and passion around every corner; when we can't think of anything but our partner; when we stay up on the phone or texting and skip sleep to write an epic love letter; when our cheeks flush in their presence, our temperatures rise, heart rates increase, and palms get sweaty—is commonly referred to as *the honeymoon stage*. During this stage it feels as though nothing can go wrong in your relationship. You overlook your partner's flaws (leaving the toilet seat up) and idiosyncrasies (forgetting to spray air freshener after using the John) because Ma Nature has clouded your mind.

## Chemistry 101

One chemical she uses for this is phenylethylamine (PEA), which acts like an amphetamine (yes, the drug). Your body reacts to PEA as it would an upper, but without the harmful side-effects and the embarrassment of failing your workplace's urine test.

Think about falling in love with your partner way back when. Do you remember feeling like you were walking on air, the cloud nine effect, tossing and turning in bed just thinking about them? You can thank PEA for those drug-like symptoms.

Another effect of PEA is the release of the chemical dopamine. This little neurotransmitter—a chemical messenger that sends text messages from one nerve cell to another in the brain—boosts both our energy levels and our motivation.

According to biological anthropologist Helen Fisher, dopamine gets us to take risks early in our relationships. It stimulates curiosity, creativity, spontaneity, and novelty-seeking.[3]

How many sixty-five-year-olds are caught each year doing it in the backseat of a Pontiac? Not many, because dopamine has been on hiatus for quite some time. (It also may have something to do with lack of flexibility.) Couples who are newly in love take risks: staying out all night clubbing, trying new sexual positions or locations, going rock climbing or bungee jumping. Risk naturally comes from dopamine early on in a relationship. Now please don't get me wrong. I've suggested that this only occurs in young couples. It doesn't. It's not about age; it's more about the newness of the relationship.

You could be a seventy-six-year-old. If you've just jumped into a new relationship, Mother Nature (or Great-Grandmother Nature, in this case) will be right there at your door doling out the chemicals and hormones associated with the honeymoon stage. Next thing you know, Grandma's entering a wet T-shirt contest in Cabo.

While we're at it, I might as well tell you about another ingredient in Mother Nature's high ball—testosterone. See, dopamine is the spigot to testosterone's faucet, and it's not just a hormone for men. Testosterone is present in women as well. It's released to prepare our bodies for intimacy. That would explain why we're so sexually active during the honeymoon stage of our relationships.

Do you wonder why we get sweaty hands, racing hearts, and become more jittery than a bunny after a double mocha latte when we first fall in love? It's due to norepinephrine, the second cousin (on his mother's side) to amphetamines, which stimulates the production of adrenaline, increasing our blood pressure when we're in the presence of that special somebody.

These chemicals create our "risk" stage in our relationship investment. But when the honeymoon stage starts to end (six to eighteen months in), Mother Nature lets us know in no uncertain terms that the lease is up on the free hormones. "All right! Everyone out of the pool!"

Next thing you know, excitement and passion take a nosedive, and we stop the risky behaviors. And that alone is not inherently "bad." The risk itself is not what we need to sustain a romantic relationship, because the next stage is called "romantic love." This feels great and secure. But it's more like a soak in a warm tub, when the honeymoon stage was like riding a wave in Kuai.

Couples often want to get back those early feelings that Mother Nature let us borrow for a few months, but we should be thankful that we're forced to move on. How could we live a sensible life with all of this constant heart-pounding, sweaty palms, sleep deprivation, and obsessive craving?

Instead of the addictive excitement of PEA and its cronies, romantic love rewards us with loyalty, comfort, stability, intimacy, dependability, and a sense of long-term commitment. Maybe our cheeks aren't flushed, but we feel comfortable and loved in this next phase, mainly because of endorphins.

Endorphins are the neurotransmitters our brains release to reward us for good behavior. You'll recognize endorphins. You know those times when no matter how hard you try to control it, every little thing makes you laugh? Those are endorphins. Ever make love, find it's the greatest sensation you've ever felt, and pray that it will never stop? Endorphins at work. You win a competition. You finished a great work out. You feel like you can conquer the world. Endorphins. Endorphins. Endorphins.

When my wife, Mary, was at the hospital ready to deliver our second child, Maya, her water broke and she had an incredibly intense contraction. When it was over she announced, "The baby's coming."

Our doula got the bed ready and prompted Mary to lie down. Conserving her energy, Mary grunted, "No. Stand." Facing me and using my body for stability, Mary clamped her hands on my shoulders like nutcrackers on a couple of pecans. I'd never seen my wife like this before. She was growling and grunting and snarling like a defensive lineman, standing, then squatting, then standing.

It was the most incredible light in which to have seen my wife. She brought Maya into the world standing. I caught the baby. And when it was over, Mary leaned back on a footstool, holding our daughter, smiling from ear to ear. She looked up at me and said, "I feel incredible. I could definitely do that again." Those, my friends, are endorphins!

How do you get these buggers firing back in your brain (without having to deliver another baby)? There are lots of ways. The easiest is through touch—lots of it. When you touch your partner in a loving way, they release oxytocin. Now, oxytocin is just a phenomenal little guy. It's been called the "hormone of love," "the foundation of romance," and even "the key to lasting relationships." And get this: it affects both men and women, an equal opportunity chemical. Not bad, eh?

Oxytocin allows us to bond with the ones we love. Instead of insomniac thoughts of our love interest, we feel peacefully warm, loving, and affectionate toward our partners. The release of oxytocin is often triggered by touch: a hug, a back massage, even a gentle brush on the neck. These are some of the simple daily investments mentioned in chapter five. But the hormone can also respond to other types of cues: a whisper in the ear, a song on the radio, or a pleasant fragrance.

When oxytocin is doing its job, we feel the need to romantically and intimately touch the ones we love, which, in turn, releases the flow of the hormone in our partners. Suddenly they feel the need to touch us. And before you know it, you've got a perpetual-motion machine fueled by the cuddle chemical.

Oxytocin increases our passion and romance. It stimulates testosterone flow (which might temporarily make us feel like we're back in the honeymoon stage). Because of oxytocin, scientists claim that people experience less tension and better moods for a full twenty-four hours after intercourse, but *not* after masturbation. It's not the orgasm. It's the touch that releases the oxytocin. (So, mathematically speaking, you could remain perpetually stress-free and happy-go-lucky if you have daily sex. Note to self: "Show wife this page in book.") Most important, oxytocin releases more endorphins, our prize for staying in love for so long.

## Risky Business

Wow, you made it through my science lesson for the day. But what the heck does this have to do with investing and risk? Here's the skinny. Although romantic love is warm and comforting and kum-baya and all, the passion and excitement will add to your relationship portfolio like buying shares of Apple stock in 1976. It's the risk—the opportunity to buy low and hit it out of the everlasting park.

Remember how norepinephrine stimulated the production of adrenaline? Well taking risks again is another way to stimulate adrenaline. Don't forget: it's not so much the risk we're after, but the affects of that risk, the bringing back of the hormones generated in the honeymoon stage.

When you do something risky together, it not only releases adrenaline, but it increase your heart rate (see "honeymoon stage"), creates exhilaration, heightens connectivity with your partner, and creates shared fear, which elevates dopamine levels and can stimulate your sex drive. In other words, it brings you closer together as a couple.

## Perceived Danger

"Okay, Mr. Fancy-Pants Romance Guru, what are some examples of creating risk?" I'm glad you asked! I don't want you to do anything stupid or dangerous. No taking ecstasy. No Russian roulette. Try some activities together that get you out of your comfort zone with *perceived* danger: riding a roller coaster, mountain climbing, bungee jumping, or river rafting (okay, maybe some of these are a wee bit dangerous). You don't have to be a triathlete or outdoors enthusiast to feel the risk. You just need to find something to get your heart pumping.

As you know, I jump-started my wife and my Romantic Adventures again after having our second child (see chapter six). As a result, one of the annual investments I'd created, I named "Three in '07." For Valentine's Day I gave my wife a card and vowed to spring three romantic surprises on her that year. She wouldn't know what they would be, when they would be coming, or how they would unfold. She just knew there would be three, and I had ten months to pull them off.

The first surprise came the following week. My wife and I played hooky (see last chapter); I simply put her in the car and we started driving. This alone started to increase our risk factor. Playing hooky is deemed *naughty*, and she was on an adventure, having to trust me fully, not knowing where I we were going.

We ended up at a Six Flags Amusement Park. It was the first time in ten or fifteen years that the two of us had visited an amusement park without kids. What did we do? We hit all the rides we hadn't been on in eons, because our girls had been too young. We rode things that dropped 1,000 feet and took rides that traveled faster than the speed of light. We dropped off buildings and were flipped around and turned upside down. We screamed, held up our hands, banged our heads on safety bars, and felt virtually like the ingredients in a fruit smoothie in a blender. And we loved it!

All those thrills and chills got our hearts pumping, our adrenaline flowing, and connected us in ways we hadn't in a long time. The perceived risk of those roller coasters and thrill rides made us feel young and alive, because we shared them together.

Between loop-de-loops and being dangled over moats filled with hungry crocodiles, Mary and I couldn't stop talking, smiling, and holding hands. We talked about the rides and made fun of one another for screaming and looking terrified, but we also talked about our past, present, and future. We people-watched and we hugged and we smooched. Before we left the park that day, I bought season passes for the entire family. With and without children, my wife and I put ourselves in perceived risk no less than nine times in 2007. The longer you are together, the more risk you need to face as a couple. It brings that honeymoon stage right back up the frontal cortex of your mind (or maybe it's the hypothalamus . . . either way, no worries; it makes you feel excited and passionate again).

A couple I spoke with not long ago took my advice about taking risks maybe a little beyond what I suggest (at least legally). They wanted to pump up the fear factor by having some semi-public sex.

They had the idea of driving to a public parking garage, finding a secluded corner, and messing around in the car.

The couple arrived at a parking garage at a local mall on a weekday and drove to the roof, assuming no one would park there when so many other open spaces were available on the lower levels. When they got to the top they noticed a car parked in the corner, the very same spot they would have chosen for *their* risky interaction. Upon closer examination, they noticed that there were people in the car—a couple to be exact. Now they didn't drive so close to know for sure, but from the positioning, the foot on the dash, and the rocking motion of the car, they surmised that this couple not only took their "risk" location, but also had stolen their activity! They were dumbfounded.

It just goes to show you that couples everywhere are finding ways to add a little risk to their relationship portfolios.

## Time Travel

That brings me to another way to fool Mother Nature into temporarily giving you your brain chemical fix. My advice: go back in time. No need for a DeLorean or flux capacitor for this, my friends. See, the brain is a complicated mass of synapses and neurons, but it's easily reminded of the past. You can simply trick your brain into bringing you back to your honeymoon stage, allowing it to release those hormones of yesteryear once again, at least for a little while. Have you ever gotten a whiff of a smell that brought you back to your childhood, or heard a song that took you back to a specific high school dance? It's amazing how that works; you might as well use it to benefit your relationship.

How do you do that? Go back and revisit some of the significant spots where you dated. Go online and listen to songs released the year you were married. Rent the first movie you two ever watched together. You'll get a lot of "oh yeah" moments. Memories start popping up. Discussing them brings you both back to an earlier, probably more exciting, time in your relationship. Then your brain will start releasing those old hormones and suddenly you're reliving the passion and excitement of years-gone-by.

A friend of mine, Vance, first kissed his wife, Selina, at a U2 concert in 1990. Eight years later, they had moved out of state and were struggling with their new jobs and new environment, being thousands of miles from family and trying to build a new circle of friends.

One night, Selina arrived home from work at 9:00 p.m. As she took her keys out and approached their apartment, she saw a sign on the door: "U2—One Night Only, March 18, 1990." With piqued interest and a baffled grin, she fumbled with the keys, hearing what she thought was the song, "Where the Streets Have No Name" on the other side of the door.

When she walked into the apartment, it was filled with people . . . of sorts. The chairs and lamps and TV, and even the dog, were dressed in clothes, all facing one wall of the apartment that had been cleaned out and had a huge strip of butcher paper taped to it (except for the dog, who stumbled to meet her at the door). On the paper was Vance's hand-drawn rendition of the band performing at a concert (just a notch above stick figures). There were names for each band member with arrows pointing at the drawings to identify who was who.

And from the "crowd" came Vance wearing a very 1990s ensemble. He greeted his wife, yelling above the band, "You made it, Selina. I saved a spot for you up front. Come on!"

Selina smiled and played right along. The two, kind of as they had eight years before, sat on their shag carpet and stared at the drawings of Bono, Adam Clayton, and the others. They listened to the concert, sipping their drinks and munching snacks, as they got closer to one another, snuggling in "the cold" and finally reliving their first kiss.

Later both Selina and Vance would go on to tell me that, although they knew it was not a true concert in 1990, the feelings of that memorable night returned, and they fell in love all over again.

Ultimately what you're trying to do here is trick your brain into giving you tastes of that honeymoon stage again. As you travel farther from the beginning of your relationship, you'll need to work on fooling your brain more often. If that means going back in time, playing hooky, or creating risk in your relationship, just know that you'll need to increase and invest more in this sector the longer you are in a relationship.

## *Portfolio-Stretching Exercise #1*

1. Think about some perceived risks you might want to share with your partner. They can be activities you've done before, or they can be brand new.

2. Work together on this exercise and start listing the perceived risks. This is a brainstorming activity, so don't shun any of your partner's ideas, and don't censor your own. Don't hold back. Throw out any idea that comes to mind. Even if it's something you know you two will never do. That idea may inspire the next, which may be the "risk idea of the century."

3. Here are some ideas to get your list started:
   - ride thrill rides at a local amusement park
   - make love in the backyard
   - go river rafting
   - try rock climbing
   - bungee jump

4. When you've exhausted all your ideas, cross off those you both agree you're not interested in. Circle the ones you would both consider, and do nothing to the ideas that only one of you would consider.

5. Attach this list to your monthly date ideas. Every now and then, pick a circled idea from the list for a date (a monthly investment). Feel free to add more to your list, and cross off or circle the ones that were in limbo.

## *Portfolio-Stretching Exercise #2*

1. As a couple, rewind your brains' memory tapes and start discussing some significant events or memories of your relationship's past. Pull out some old photos to help inspire you if you think it will help.

2. You may want to consider places you've visited or frequented (the first place you kissed, the place you got engaged or married, the club you went to every Saturday night when you were dating), songs that were important ("your song," the first song you danced to), or movies and TV shows you used to watch (the movie you went to on your first date, the TV show you would never miss while you were engaged).

3. Go over the list together. Decide which idea you want to utilize in the creation of your go-back-in-time date. Then, start to design it. When was it? Where will you be? What music or clothes will you need? What was significant about this? Now pencil it on your calendar as one of your monthly date investments.

4. Now go have some fun and get your honeymoon stage back!

## Key Points for Investing: Assess the Risks

✓ Unlike finances, in relationships you want to add more risk the longer you invest.

✓ Risk brings you back to the honeymoon stage.

✓ The honeymoon stage is filled with hormones, chemicals, and neurotransmitters that make us feel excited and passionate.

✓ After the "honeymoon stage" we must *work* to get it back.

✓ You really don't need to do anything dangerous. "Perceived risk" is just as powerful.

✓ Go back in time and relive the past.

**Notes**

1. *Getting the Facts of Saving and Investing*, US Securities Exchange Commission, 2007, 12.
2. *The Eight Biggest Mistakes Investors Make*, Fisher Investments, 5.
3. *20/20*, ABC, January 31, 2009.

— CHAPTER EIGHT —

# MAINTAIN GOOD CREDIT

*I*n the world of finance exists a very important word: *credit*. Why is credit so important? Because if you've got good credit, banks, lenders, American Express, and coffee barristers trust you. If your credit is not so hot, people look down their noses at you. Institutions think twice about letting you get your mitts on their cash. And if you are allowed the privilege of loan-status, you'll be charged loan shark interest rates. This will put you further into debt, forcing you to stop reading the book at this point and turn back to chapter three, "Get Rid of Your Debt," when all you truly want to do is read the next five chapters.

Good credit makes the world of money go round. It proves you are worthy of a loan should you ever need one. And loans are a part of our culture. They're not inherently bad. We use loans to buy houses, cars, and for higher education. We borrow every time we use a credit card. Before a financial institution forks over any cash, they will determine at what interest rate you'll repay the loan. That rate is based on your credit score. Your credit score reflects your financial responsibility. If you have a history of paying your debt on time and in full, your credit score will be higher than if you have a history of borrowing more than you can repay, not paying your cable bill on time, and having filed chapter eleven three years ago.

Therefore, you need to always work on your financial credit score by spending less than you earn, paying your bills in full and on time, as well as proving yourself a sound financial investment for the loan institutions.

How does good credit apply to relationships? You'll want good credit in case you ever need to take out a loan from your relationship portfolio.

What do I mean by "a relationship loan"? There will be times in every long-term, committed relationship where you make a blunder: you forget your partner's birthday; you come home an hour late without calling first; or you buy your husband the complete *Sex in the City* DVD set for your anniversary. When you blow it (and we all do at some point), you need to backpedal, ask for forgiveness, essentially, take out a loan. You're asking your relationship institution (your partner) to help you out of a tough spot by offering a little leeway. Depending upon your credit score, your partner will determine how much interest to charge you.

What's "interest" in this case? The length of time it takes for you to be forgiven; the number of nights you must sleep on the couch; and how often the incident can be used in future squabbles. Essentially, how long you are in the proverbial "doghouse." Of course, you want to have proven yourself responsible in your relationship to maximize your credit rating so as to minimize your interest rate when the inevitable occurs.

Take this quick, five-question relationship credit quiz to see what your credit score is:

**1) Fidelity**
When was the last time you cheated on a partner?
    a. Never
    b. A prior relationship
    c. Early on in this relationship
    d. Within the last two months

**2) Honesty**
How do you feel about lying to your partner?
    a. Should never do it
    b. White lies are fine
    c. I lie occasionally to him/her
    d. Just a way of life

### 3) Flirtation

How often do you flirt with someone other than your partner?
    a. Never
    b. Occasionally, but I let him/her know I'm attached
    c. Often
    d. Often, in the hopes of it leading to more

### 4) Trust

Do you trust your partner?
    a. Yes, fully
    b. Mostly, but I have peeked at his/her text messages once or twice
    c. Somewhat, yet I regularly read his/her emails without him/her knowing
    d. No, I sign on to his/her Facebook account and pretend that I am him/her

### 5) Money

How do you feel about the money you share with your partner?
    a. What's mine is ours
    b. Sometimes I stash a bit aside without him/her knowing
    c. I don't always share my purchases with my partner
    d. What's mine is mine and what's theirs is mine: the person with the most money wins

### Scoring Your Credit Quiz

Start with the number 900. For every "a", your score remains unchanged. For every "b" subtract 40. For every "c" subtract 80. And subtract 120 points for each "d" you chose.

Your credit score will run between 300 and 900, with 900 being the optimal score. A score of 300 tells you your interest rate will be the highest—if your partner is even willing to give you a loan.

### Excellent (800–900)

You are in terrific standing with your relationship institution. You have excellent credit, are well-trusted, and should be able to qualify for the lowest interest rates.

### Good (700–799)

You are in good standing with your relationship institution. You have relatively good credit and are trusted. If you find yourself in need of a loan, you should be able to pay it off in a comfortable amount of time due to the interest rate you will earn.

### Fine (600–699)

You have squeaked by as a borrower who is not quite "high risk," but you are on the watch list. The relationship institution is keeping an eye on you. If you step out of line, you could easily become a "high risk" borrower, which will bump up your interest rates, making repaying your loan difficult.

### Poor (500–599)

You are officially a "high risk" borrower. Your relationship institution is vigilantly watching you. One more slip up means your interest rate will go through the roof, and you will need a lot of time to get yourself back in the black again.

### Bad (400–499)

You are a huge liability. Not many relationship institutions will be willing to give you any type of loan, and with your history, it's pretty much a guarantee that you are going to screw up again. When you do, you may end up out on your ears for quite some time, if not indefinitely.

### Laughed Right Out of the Institution (300–399)

Sorry, but you are in trouble, my friend. You are in the lowest of all credit scores. You have proven yourself completely unworthy. Any relationship institution that values *their* reputation will not even consider offering you a loan, at any interest rate. You're what's known as "bad debt" because your history has proven you never repay your loans. The only possible way for you to take out a new loan is to find a partner who has incredibly low self-esteem, or go groveling on your knees to your present relationship institution and start paying "cash." Do what is necessary to rebuild your relationship without asking for anything in return, and start rebuilding your credit score *today*!

The best way to rebuild your credit is by proving to your partner that you are fully committed and 100 percent faithful in terms of your relationship. In other words, no cheating! If you have a past history of being "faithfully-challenged," expect no mercy from the relationship institution when it's time to take a loan.

Of course no couples get into relationships expecting infidelity, but according to *The Journal of Couple and Relationship Therapy*, half of all married women and three-fifths of married men will have an affair during their marriages.[1] Somewhere along the line, we screw up our credit score, but exactly what happened? It's rarely something catastrophic that causes us to "wander." It's more than likely boredom, routine, loss of attraction, less sex, or decreased passion and excitement, as well as just a "going-through-the-motions humdrum" existence. In other words, the romance is gone.

## Temptation

Behavioral economists have identified a major reason why some people cannot save their money, spend more than they have, and ruin their credit: temptation. Although we know we shouldn't, we too often buy on impulse—a big sale on toilet bowl plungers or angora socks—or we purchase stuff to temporarily make us "feel better," even though we know we'll end up paying for it later.[2]

Do you see the relationship parallels? Why do we have affairs? Temptation. We know it's wrong and risky, and if we're caught, we're in deep donkey doo. Yet, 50 percent to 60 percent of us will do it anyway. Impulse. We think we'll feel better. But in the end, an affair is the same as deliberately trashing our relationship score.

Behavioral economists tell us that the solution to this temptation problem is to make saving more fun than *not* spending. As you remember from chapter 6, not spending is a passive act, whereas saving is a choice, a decision that is conscious and deliberate. Neuro-economist Ben Seymour of University College, London, has studied brain scans of human guinea pigs whose brains, when merely imagining a future purchase, nearly reacted the same as actually buying the item.[3]

The same methodology can be applied to your relationship. When things become drab and blah in your relationship, don't give into temptation. Instead, make your current relationship just as much fun and exciting as a potential affair. J.D. Roth, finance author and editor of the blog getrichslowly.org, warns folks that they get into financial trouble when they think they need the latest gadget or toy. Instead, he says we should look around us at what we already have and use those items. Find happiness in what's already ours, instead of feeling the constant need for something new and different to bring us happiness.[4] The same applies to your relationship. Take what you already have and learn to appreciate your partner again.

Think about it. An affair takes a lot of effort, time, and planning. (Even if it's an affair on impulse, it's been in the planning stages for a long time.) And we justify it by telling ourselves that something is missing from our relationship. Although an affair might bring you back to the honeymoon stage (it feels good, exciting, and intense), it doesn't fix your relationship, and eventually when the dust settles and the affair is done, you'll be worse off in your present relationship than before the affair.

If you expend the same energy on your current relationship to jump-start it, you will avoid a major drop in your credit score. What can you do to counter temptation? You've read many ideas in previous chapters—go on dates, romantic adventures, make a resolution, take the 52-Week Challenge, connect daily, play hooky, take some perceived risks—and there will be more ideas later.

## Changes in the Bedroom

One of the aspects of an affair that appears very appealing is the sexual side. Sex in long-term, committed relationships tends to become stale and routine: same night, same bed, same position, same partner, twenty minutes (if you're lucky) in the same dark bedroom, once a week.

Adding spice to your sex life is a great way to keep from straying in your relationship. Start changing things around. Consider any of the following based on your (meaning you *and* your partner's) level of comfort: a new location, more foreplay, different time of day, increased frequency, new positions. Be sure to prep for your sexual excursions every now and then: shave, shower, style your hair, and put on a little make-up or cologne. Think about how you would want to be perceived if you *were* having an affair. You want to be as desirable as you can. So prep for an affair with your partner.

Try to last a little longer. Maybe turn on the lights, for goodness sake. Read something a little racy, watch a DVD that might stimulate your senses, or use a feather to heighten each other's nerve endings. What will put spice back into your lovemaking? Consider undressing one another. Instead of taking off your own clothes, make disrobing a part of the sex act itself. It slows things down, builds excitement, and necessitates touching and caressing, which we know does the whole oxytocin-thing (see last chapter). When you're in the honeymoon stage (or having an affair) and you know that you'll probably be having sex later on, it makes the entire day exciting. What can you do now to keep you excited about having sex with your partner later tonight?

There's a couple, Alyssa and Barry, who loved role-playing. They used it to keep temptation at bay while making their relationship as much fun as an affair, thus never having to be unfaithful.

They would play masseuse and client, golf instructor and paying customer, and even prostitute and John. They kept clothes that they might have otherwise donated to Goodwill in their closet to use, so during role-play, they could literally tear it off of one another. The most elaborate "temptation-buster" they would periodically play was a bit intricate. They would create roles for one another, book a hotel room out of town, then take separate cars and "meet for the first time" at a bar or coffee shop. Small talk would lead to flirtation, which would lead to sexual connotations and eventually a trip back to Barry's rented hotel for a "one-night stand." These two didn't need an affair.

Basically, as a couple you need to find the strength to avoid "impulse buys." "Window shopping" is fine, healthy, and natural. In financial terms window-shopping is browsing through potentially risky products without actually investing. In a relationship, it's noticing an attractive person and admiring him or her. Even sexual thoughts about another are common, fine, and healthy. But don't become obsessed or act on unfaithful thoughts.

## Fantasy and Flirtation

Fleeting sexual thoughts are common and fine, and you shouldn't feel guilty as long as you don't become obsessed or act on them. Many couples incorporate a variation of their fantasies in their sexual play to feel the excitement and exhilaration without actually fulfilling the fantasy.

Flirtation is a trickier fence to walk. There are different levels of flirtation. And partners can react differently to them. If you have a strong relationship and someone flirts with you a bit, it can feel good and be an ego-booster. But it's important not to overstep relational boundaries, nor lead the person on. If you're not sure, err on the conservative side.

About ten years ago, a guy at my wife's work always complimented her about her green eyes. Of course my wife was flattered, but she made sure he knew she was married by saying, "My husband tells me that as well." The guy realized she was committed to me and any further flirtation was merely for fun.

Good credit and interest rates in finance and relationships basically come down to trust. Do I trust you enough to let you borrow money? Do I trust you'll be faithful to me? Trust is a tricky thing. It can take an instant to lose and an eternity to get back.

You can have years of a happy, trusting relationship where honesty and faithfulness reign. But one little indiscretion—ranging from an inappropriate phone message to a full-blown affair, depending upon your particular partner—can ruin everything in a heartbeat. One lie, one sneaky move, one inappropriate text message, one kiss, one night in someone else's bed—it's best to keep trust held in highest esteem in your relationship.

I love what Michelle Singletary, personal finance columnist for *The Washington Post* and author of *The Power to Prosper: 21 Days to Financial Freedom* says is her best money-saving advice. It came from her grandmother: ask yourself if you need it or just want it. "Whenever she went shopping, she asked herself whether something was a need or a want. I do this—and just about every time, I end up putting back or scaling down what I have."[5] I do believe that love and a strong healthy relationship is truly a *need*. So before you stray from your relationship, ask yourself, *Is this a need or a want?* If you think that cheating is a need, chances are you've been neglecting what you already have. You need to invest in what you already have before you lose it.

## *Portfolio-Stretching Exercise* 💕 _____

(See Worksheet 10)

1. Time to have an illicit affair with your partner. I want you both to feel the animal desire that you once had (and may still have) so that your credit score stays in the "excellent" range.

2. Think about your bedroom antics lately. By yourself, determine what would make sex even more exciting. Let your mind drift back to the beginning of your relationship. What's changed in the bedroom? What about your fantasies? Are there any that you would like to see as realities?

3. Look at the following list. On a sheet of paper, separate from your spouse, determine what areas you would like to see some changes:

   | | | |
   |---|---|---|
   | foreplay | role-playing | toys |
   | length of session | racy literature | time of day |
   | location | visual stimulation | frequency |

   (If there are areas not covered on this list that you're interested in, feel free to add them.)

4. For each topic you've written, list changes you think would add more passion and excitement to your intimacy.

**Example:** Under "Location" you might list:

| | |
|---|---|
| in the shower | on a hiking trail |
| kitchen table | our car |
| the backyard | elevator |
| the garage | and so on |

5. Once you have your list, circle all of the ideas you think your partner may want to try. Do *not* cross off the others, though.

6. Time to come together and compare. Share your lists of circled items with one another and be sure to discuss, explain, and clarify. Communication is key. When you're entering uncharted sexual territory, it's important to be open and clear with one another.

*Key Points for Investing:*
*Maintain Good Credit*

✓ Good credit guarantees you a low interest rate when making a loan.

✓ In relationships, we take out loans from our partners when we make a blunder.

✓ A good credit history means no infidelity and being honest.

✓ The best way to beat temptation is to make your relationship as much fun as, if not more than, an affair.

✓ Bringing excitement to both your relationship and an affair takes lots of time and effort, but only the former offers long-term dividends.

✓ One way to combat temptation is to change your sexual routine.

✓ Fantasy and flirtation are not inherently bad for a relationship . . . just be careful.

✓ Hold trust in high esteem.

✓ Ask yourself if you need it or just want it.

## Notes

1. Lindsay Shugarman, "Percentage of Married Couples Who Cheat," http://www.catalogs.com/info/relationships/percentage-of-married-couples-who-cheat-on-each-ot.html.
2. Tim Harford, "How to Save Smarter," *Parade Magazine*, May 10, 2009, 10.
3. Ibid.
4. Mary Hunt, "The Best Money Advice You'll Ever Get," *Woman's Day Magazine*, February 17, 2010, 106.
5. Ibid.

— CHAPTER NINE —

# GET YOUR KIDS ON THE RIGHT PATH

We invest for many reasons: for unforeseen, costly future events; to buy a home or car; or to prepare for retirement. But one of the most important reasons many of us save is to invest and build a financial portfolio for our offspring. We want to finance their higher education, pay for their weddings, get them their first cars, help them purchase homes, and even leave them little nest eggs when we are no longer around.

Give a kid a buck, he'll spend for a day. Teach him how to save and he'll spend for a lifetime. Studies show us that when children have been exposed to money, given an allowance, and taught about saving and compounding interest, they are less likely to run into financial turmoil as adults.[1]

Anything our folks do regularly sticks with us. "Set a good example for your kids," Jan Dahlin Geiger tells us in *Get Your Assets In Gear*.[2] "They will learn much more from what you do than what you say." We either grow up to become our folks or their polar opposites.

The *FDIC Consumer News* tells parents to "show and tell" when it comes to kids and managing money. Discuss value and need (versus desire) while shopping. Take them to the bank and explain the products and services. Model responsible bill paying behavior and talk about credit, credit cards, and interest.[3]

83

Our actions have an incredible impact on our children. No matter how much they may want to rebel and push away, parents are their role models in so many ways. Our customs, rituals, and routines become their ways of life in adulthood. Being responsible with money while our children are young is crucial for their financial success in the future.

In my home, both my ten-year-old and five-year-old receive weekly allowance for their chores. They have savings accounts and understand how that money grows. My wife and I invest in mutual funds and 529 college plans for them. My oldest daughter invests in a different stock every year. We also have our own currency at home used to reward, to charge, and for purchasing items and activities. My wife and I are confident we've built a solid financial knowledge-based foundation for our daughters' futures.

## The Parental Impact

When I was a teenager and would finish washing the dishes, my mom always yelled from the living room, "Did you wipe down the counter?"

Wipe down the counter? I'm washing the dishes here, not cleaning the kitchen. As I ran the sponge over the yellow linoleum counter of our little home, exasperated, I'd holler back, "Yes, Mom." Then I grumbled under my breath, "Dishes are dishes. Counters are counters. When I grow up, I'll never ask my kids to clean the counter if they're supposed to be washing dishes."

It's twenty-five years later. I've got my own sink, my own dirty dishes, and my own yellow linoleum counters. I find myself walking into the kitchen to an empty sink with clean dishes drip-drying in the rack (yes, we are old school—no dishwasher). Where do I look next? That's right. The counter.

"Who washed the dishes but didn't wipe down the counter?!" I yell. Holy smokes! I've become my mother!

This example applies to relationships as well. Look at the relationship you're in now. There's a good chance it's a lot like your parents'; if not, it's probably at the opposite end of the spectrum.

As you know from the first chapter, calling my parents' marriage "rocky" would be an understatement. They loved one another but couldn't keep romance alive; they married each other twice and divorced each other twice. I am *certain* this is why I have become a relationship expert and America's Romance Guru. I am *sure* that my parents' relationship molded me in such a way that romance is, and always has been, integral in my relationships. I am *positive* I can thank them for the strong, loving, and healthy relationship I have with my wife today. We either become our parents (counter-wiper) or become the Bizarro World version of them. I was fortunate because I didn't repeat their relationship mistakes. I took the "180-degree" route, but sadly most won't. Most of us will just repeat what we saw our parents do, good or bad.

Let your kids see the love and romance you've been learning. It's not only okay, but advisable, to let them see you holding hands, sneaking a smooch, tickling one another, and saying "I love you." It makes children feel safe, secure, and nurtured in family structures. A 2009 study published by the US Department of Health and Human Services found that "the quality of a child's parents' marriage had as much influence on his or her future mental and physical health and well-being as his or her own relationship with either parent."[4]

The little ones will want to jump right in there with you, sharing a hug or being part of the tickle battle. The teens, on the other hand, may scoff and tell you to get a room, but they will also feel as though their family unit is strong, so they can focus on other important aspects of teen life, like school, sports, text messaging, and learning to survive the pigsty they call a room.

Also be sure to involve your children in date nights. No, I don't mean ask permission or take them with you. Instead, be sure they know ahead of time when you and your partner are going out. Let them see that parents need "play dates" too and that alone time is crucial and normal for couples. They may complain at first (or not), but as long as you continue to date consistently, it'll just become a way of life, like brushing your teeth and shaving the cat. When your children grow up and are in committed, long-term relationships, they too will incorporate all they learned from you, not to mention the security they'll feel knowing that Mom and Dad are a close, loving couple.

## The Family Structure's Foundation

You and your partner are the foundation of your family structure. Every structure needs a strong foundation to ensure stability. Your relationship with your partner is the most important relationship in your family.

Whenever I say this statement in a crowded room, hands shoot up; I get many letters and emails from folks who tell me that the most important connection in a family is between parent and child. Although a crucial and important bond, that between parent and child is *not* the most important. "The most important relationship in any family is the marital one, and the best thing parents can do for their children is to love one another,"[5] says clinical social worker Daniel L. Buccino. The parent-child bond is like the framing of a house (going back to the whole home structure metaphor here). You can have terrific and strong framing, but it means nothing if the foundation is cracked or weak. Mom and Dad's relationship is that foundation.

I met a man named Brent not long ago at a dinner party. In his late thirties and a professional type, Brent owned a realty company. He showed me pictures of his beautiful wife and two darling daughters, and he was very well-spoken and educated. As we chatted and he found out what I did, he opened up to me. "Leon," he said in a low tone, "my wife and I are having trouble. We're currently in couples therapy."

Not the couple most would suspect having marital issues. "Why are you two seeing a therapist?" I asked.

"Because we lost touch with each other," he admitted.

Brent told me that when he and his wife became parents, the bond between the two of them became secondary to the new bonds being forged between them and their daughters. They lost the needle of their relationship in the haystack of parenthood. There were no fights, no resentment, and no infidelity. Instead there was a couple living in the same house, communicating about who's going to pick up Kaitlyn after gymnastics practice and if Courtney had her lunch money and nothing about, "How was your day?" or "When's our next date night?"

They lived in the same home but were growing apart, becoming strangers, under the same roof. Their bonds with their children were strong and secure, but their marital foundation was cracking. Do you think the kids noticed? Absolutely. Did they feel that they were a part of a strong, secure family unit? No. What did this tell the children about their own future relationships? They could potentially enter relationships with fear of where their relationships may end.

Watching parental relationships is the training ground for a child's own future relationships. If the child does not learn ways to express love from Mom and Dad, he will tend to have difficulty with expressing love when it's his turn. Unless the child is aware enough to ride the pendulum to the other side, he is destined to repeat his parents' relationship errors in adulthood.

## Fight Right

You'll also help your children by letting them see you disagree. Many parents vow never to argue in front of their children. If arguing means name-calling, yelling, and hitting below the belt or in the eye socket, then behind closed doors is the way to go. (FYI: behind closed doors or not, that kind of fighting is detrimental to your relationship and will erode it like the Colorado River through the Grand Canyon).

If you fight fair, it shows your children how to handle conflict resolution in life and future relationships in a healthy and succinct way. Children who do not know how to handle conflict in their relationships will be destined to frustration in their own marriages. Some of the ten rules to follow in "How to Fight Fair in Marriage,"[6] an article by Simon Presland, include "Avoid personal insults and character assassination," meaning deal with the subject at hand and avoid low-blows, and "Confront with truth. Affirm with love." This means start with a positive followed up with your concern: "I love that you are helping your partner through a tough time at work, but when you're running late, I'd feel much better if you'd give me a call to let me know." My favorite is number ten: "Confront to heal, not to win." If you are confronting your partner in front of your children, make sure they understand the goal of the confrontation is to make the relationship *better*, not to be victorious with a knockout punch and prove you are right.

Harmony, not dissonance, is the goal when you confront. Let

your children learn this skill and allow them to see that you two can come together and still love one another, even when you don't agree.

Show, don't tell, your children what a loving relationship looks like, and you'll be starting their junior relationship portfolios with sizable deposits.

## *Portfolio-Stretching Exercise*

This chapter's portfolio-stretching activity is really meant for couples who have children living with them at home. If this doesn't apply to you, feel free to skip the activity. However, you may want to read it anyway, just to be sure you received every penny's worth that you spent on the book. (If you got it as a gift . . . eh, go ahead and skip it.)

This is a pretty simple activity.

1. With your partner, list ways you could express love and romance appropriately in front of your children. The list might include saying, "I love you," holding hands when you all go out, dancing in the kitchen, kissing good-bye, going out on dates, coming home with flowers, and so on.

2. Make a point of exposing your children to great modeling of a loving relationship at least once a day.

3. If you want to challenge yourself, up the ante and shoot for three or four times a day, whatever feels comfortable and right with your family dynamics.

4. Rinse and repeat.

## Key Points for Investing:
## Get Your Kids on the Right Path

✓ The relationship between Mom and Dad is the foundation to the family structure.

✓ Children learn relationship skills from the adults they live with.

✓ Model strong, loving, and romantic expressions for your children.

✓ The little ones will want to be a part of it. The older ones may scoff. But all of them will feel a sense of security, safety, and reliability.

### Notes

1. Salma Jafri, "How To Help Kids Become Debt-Free Adults," http://personalbudgeting.suite101.com/article.cfm/how_to_help_kids_become_debtfree_adults, October 1, 2009.
2. Jan Dahlin Geiger, *Get Your Assets In Gear* (Outskirts Press, 2007).
3. "Money Tips for All Ages," FDIC Consumer News, Spring 2008, 9.
4. Jenna McCarthy, "What Kids Learn From Your Marriage," *Parents Magazine*, 94.
5. Ibid.
6. Simon Presland, "How to Fight Fair In Marriage," http://www.lifetoolsforwomen.com/f/fight-fair.htm.

# Chapter Ten

# REINVEST
# YOUR PORTFOLIO

*I*f we can get what we want, we're satisfied. If we can get it faster, that's even better. That's the ideology behind the success of McDonald's, Polaroid cameras, CNN, and the Internet. Get what I want now instead of later, and I'm happy.

When we watch our investment portfolios grow slowly, we're satisfied, but if there's a sudden spike in our investments and we can reap the dividends, we're meeting our financial goals even faster; hence the huge toothy grins on our windfallen faces.

What's one way to get our portfolio to grow quicker? Warren Buffett tells us (and I would be listening when the richest dog in the pound barks) to reinvest the profits.[1] Too many of us want to celebrate our growth by spending what we've gained. Instead, reinvest your profits and allow your gain (not just your initial investment) to make more money for you. Here's a hypothetical example: you stick one grand in a CD that kicks back a 3 percent return at year's end. Now, you've got an extra thirty bucks. Leave your initial thousand in your CD to reap another 3 percent return, but take your 30 dollars (which is really not a risk, because if you lose it, your initial $1,000 investment remains untouched and is getting you a guaranteed return), and buy a stock with it. If the stock tanks, *c'est la vie*. If it doubles, take half of it (thirty dollars again) and plop it into a mutual fund. Do you see what's happening here? Your money is making money, while your initial investment stays in a product with a guaranteed return. Only your gains are used in a little riskier investment with a heavier return.

I have a ten-year-old daughter who started her own business when she was seven. She took out a loan from the Bank of Mama and Papa. She bought supplies and created a manufacturing business called Maddie's Monkey Business. Check it out online (MaddiesMonkeyBusiness.com). She learned quickly about profits and expenses, being in the red as opposed to the black. Soon she was using terms like "entrepreneur," "advertising," "reinvesting," and more.

After a few weeks, this second grader had paid back her loan (she paid it quickly enough so as to accrue no interest) and was pulling in a profit. She was in the black. The first time she realized her debt was cleared she was ecstatic, but instead of taking her profits and buying a Barbie, she reinvested right back into her business, buying new supplies and creating new lines of products.

Eventually, this young lady was able to pay herself a monthly salary (25 percent of her profits), donate to charity (10 percent of her profits), and reinvest in her business. With the extra cash flow, she decided to expand her investments and started buying stocks like Intel, Walmart, and Disney. She stepped out of her comfort zone and took a risk reinvesting her profits.

## Reinvesting in Your Relationship

How do you do this in a relationship? When your portfolio is growing because things are going well between you and your partner, there's romance and communication, excitement and security. This is when you should consider adding more to your portfolio. Diversify and let your profits work for you. Use the momentum of your growing portfolio to bring you to different sectors in your relationship. Try something new. Take a class together (covered in chapter five). Surprise your partner (chapter six). Take a trip.

Whatever you do, though, don't sit on your haunches and just celebrate what you've done. You'll need to continue to invest to keep this relationship a priority and, if you want it to grow quickly, you'll need to branch out into new sectors.

Does this mean to stop doing what worked? Heck, no. What's been working in your relationship is the equivalent of your 3 percent return on your grand. It's guaranteed. Keep it there. Now risk your thirty bucks in a new arena. If you blow it, so what? If the new sector or product doesn't get your juices flowing or causes your partner to roll his eyes, ditch it and try something else. If it works for the two of you, though, make this a regular part of your investment and realize that you are diversifying!

Don't fret over an investment that doesn't pan out now and again. Remember, you're already building wealth through those initial investments that you know are working. You reap the interest and let that interest make money for you, even when the "risky" investment falls short. That's called compounding interest.

Your initial investment gains interest. That interest *plus* your investment makes *more* interest. That new interest, plus the old *and* your initial investment make you even more. I could continue in this manner, but I assume you get the picture (if not, email me, and I'll continue until you do).

The value of an initial $1,000 investment at a 6 percent return after ten years is almost $1,800. In thirty years, you're at $5,743.[2] What this means is let what's working for you continue to work for you.

In your relationship, if going dancing every Thursday puts a smile on both your faces, that's the interest you earn. You deposit it in your relationship portfolio, but you don't stop dancing. That investment works. So go again next Thursday. That will build on the previous week's interest, making your portfolio that much richer. Keep going every Thursday as long as you keep collecting interest from this investment.

You can choose to diversify even further. You go skinny-dipping in your pool a couple times a week. If that ices your cake, you have more compounding interest. If not, no sweat. Lose the skinny-dipping; you're still collecting on the Thursday night dancing.

## Tim and Jennifer

My wife and I have some friends, Tim and Jennifer, who have been married about twenty years. Every month for I-don't-know-how-long, the couple had made it a priority to schedule regular dates two to four times a month. They also regularly have a glass of wine in their Jacuzzi every Friday night, outside under the stars. This was a time to relax and catch up with one another.

These two investments worked for them, giving them interest that has been compounding over many years. It helped create a solid, healthy, and balanced foundation for a wonderful relationship. But they weren't satisfied and wanted to reinvest some of their profits in new sectors to help build their relationship portfolio faster.

So they tried joining a coed soccer team, tried writing an erotic book, and then took a pottery class. Although fun, none of these investments caught on as had the Friday night Jacuzzi and date nights. But they didn't give up. One day they hit on a new sector that reaped enough interest to keep investing in: cooking. Every Monday, either Tim or Jen creates an appetizer and dessert, and the other makes the entrée.

They sometimes plan the meal together. Other times, it's a surprise. Cooking together in the kitchen and listening to French music really floats their corks. Sharing the meal and feeding one another is a sensual and sometimes harmonious experience that they have chosen to invest in regularly.

## Believe First

Before we go any further, let me tell you a secret about the rich, the financially successful, the folks with the impressive financial portfolios and deep pockets. The reason they got to where they are is 96.3 percent* due to attitude. Wealthy people think wealthy. They believe it. They embody it. Therefore, they live it. They set small, attainable goals and work step-by-step to achieve them, expecting positive results the entire time.

The following list can be viewed as attainable goals, your new sectors for retirement. View these ideas and date tips as deposits for an emergency fund. Add a little more to your plate. Put in a little more romantic effort here or there so when the tough times come you have something to pull from, a secret "stash account" you've been building to help the two of you ride out the obstacles that all relationships run up against.

*(margin of error +/- 2%)

Remember, to get what you want from life—be it money or love—you have to set goals and be committed to reaching them. It takes work, time, and effort, but anything worthwhile always does. Don't forget about the power of compounding interest. It works for us when we invest and against us when we are in debt. Keep your head above water, and make a wave when you can . . . just like in the old sitcom *Good Times*. As Jimmy Walker used to say, "Dy-no-mite!"

## The List

The following list can be used to diversify, reinvest, surprise, or be used as (at least) monthly dates. Change them to fit your needs. Add more if you wish.

1. Cook dinner together.

2. Go kayaking.

3. Stay in bed one day together, watch videos, snuggle, nap, and do whatever else may move you.

4. Flirt at home.

5. Flirt in public.

6. Call each other at work at least once a day to say, "I love you."

7. Make it a point to compliment one another.

8. Hug each other daily.

9. Go miniature golfing.

10. Buy a Xbox gaming console with Kinect and challenge each other to competitions.

11. Try a new restaurant monthly.

12. Take boudoir photos of one another.

13. Play strip poker.

14. Go to a department store with a small amount of cash ($5–$20) to shop for one another. Meet at the car in twenty minutes and exchange gifts.

15. Plant and upkeep your garden weekly.

16. Renew your vows (if you're not married, get married).

17. Cuddle often.

18. Eat breakfast in bed weekly.

19. Wash each other's hair.

20. Once a month pick a new location for sex.

21. Once a month pick a new position for sex.

22. Arrange scavenger hunts for one another.

23. Have a fancy meal at a fast food restaurant. Get dressed for the affair. Bring a basket with fine China, silverware, and stemware, as well as a tablecloth, linen napkins, a candle, and a vase with flowers. Spread out the tablecloth. Set out the flowers and light the candle. Place fast food on the fine China and soft drinks in your stemware. Then let everyone else wonder why.

24. Set up a candlelight bubble bath for the two of you.

25. Go skinny-dipping.

26. Circle items in a catalog you want. Exchange catalogs with your partner, and buy them surprises when they least expect it.

27. Together discuss three of your biggest wishes and work on making them come true this year.

28. Every day for the next one hundred days, write down one new reason you love your partner. Share the list when it's complete.

29. Kiss unexpectedly.

30. Kiss often.

31. Take a walk on the beach.

32. Visit a pet store together.

33. Make out until your lips go numb, like you used to.

34. Go wine tasting.

35. Dress each other before you go out.

36. Undress each other when you get back.

37. Try talking dirty.

38. Go out on another "first date." Pretend to get to know each other all over again.

39. Sit on your roof and stargaze.

40. Take a class together at the local community college.

41. Shower together.

42. Slow dance in front of the fireplace (be sure to light the fire first).

43. Make love in the kitchen.

44. Make love on the beach.

45. Make love in front of the fireplace (if it's lit, don't get too close).

46. Go away for a weekend, last minute.

47. Do a striptease for one another.

48. Have a picnic (candles, wine, blanket, the whole nine).

49. Become pen-pals with each other. Write letters and send them to each other via snail mail.

50. Have an indoor picnic (see #48)

51. Make it a point to *always* say "I love you" when you get off the phone or when departing face-to-face.

52. Go biking.

53. Go bowling.

54. Learn a new kind of art form together.

55. Hit up yard sales next weekend, and buy at least one thing for each other.

56. Go camping but bring only one sleeping bag (a two-person, preferably).

57. Tell each other something the other doesn't know about you.

58. Lick chocolate sauce off each other.

59. Wash your car together.

60. Go to an amusement park and ride the scariest rides.

61. Wake up early and watch the sun rise.

62. Get some good reading material and a blanket and cuddle on the bed or sofa together while you read separately.

63. Create a movie night: rent a DVD, pop some corn, dim the lights, and enjoy.

64. Do one of your partner's regular chores this week.

65. Once a week have a massage night. Take turns giving rubs: neck, feet, hands, back. Have towels, oils, candles, and music on hand.

66. Become Lookie-Loos. Go to some open houses (homes for sale) and dream about buying a new abode.

67. Go sailing.

68. Take a train ride locally.

69. When a band plays nearby that was popular when you two dated, get tickets to the concert.

70. Do a jigsaw puzzle together.

71. Paint a room in your house as a team.

72. Join a gym and work out together.

73. Watch each other's favorite TV shows together.

74. Take a cruise.

75. Take a trip to a place where you don't understand the language.

76. Plan a vacation on a different continent.

77. Go river rafting.

78. Relive a memorable moment early in your relationship.

79. Go to an adult store together and buy something (gum does not count).

80. Play hooky from work together.

81. Plan a weekend getaway to Las Vegas.

82. Go to a bed and breakfast.

83. Read the same book together, either to each other or, after each chapter, talk about it.

84. Buy Twister and play it.

85. Have an "all-nighter" where neither of you sleep, and focus exclusively on each other.

86. Hold hands in public.

87. Get a shoebox, a pad of paper, and a pen. Whenever you partner does anything you appreciate, write it on the paper and stick it in the shoebox. Once a week, share them together.

88. Experiment with a "no TV/computer day" once a month.

89. Go dancing.

90. Teach each other something new this month. Work on it each weekend.

91. Hunt for four-leaf clovers. The first to find one, or whoever finds the most, gets a reward from their partner.

92. Schedule dates regularly.

93. Draw pictures for each other.

94. Create and give one another love coupons (for chores, massages, and so on.) (See page 145.)

*Add your own ideas:*

95.

96.

97.

98.

99.

## *Portfolio-Stretching Exercise*

1. Together with your partner, circle the items on this list you want to try.

2. Cross off the ones you don't.

3. Do the circled ones!

   **\*Advanced activity:** when you've done all the circled activities, do the crossed off ones too.

## *Key Points for Investing: Reinvest Your Profits*

✓ Invest in new sectors of your relationship.

✓ Don't stop doing what works.

✓ If the new sector doesn't pay dividends, you've lost none of your initial capital.

✓ Envision and expect a strong and healthy relationship, then work like mad, and it will come to you.

✓ Little goals lead to big dreams.

✓ Try something new regularly.

**Notes**
1. Warren Buffett, "10 Ways to Get Rich," *Parade Magazine*, Sept. 7, 2008, 4.
2. *Savings Fitness: A Guide to Your Money and Your Financial Future*, US Department of Labor, 17.

# Chapter Eleven

# IT IS TIME TO HIRE A PROFESSIONAL

$\mathscr{S}$ome people "get" finances. They understand the market. Inflation and cost-of-living increases make sense to them. They know the difference between tax-deferred investing and tax-exempt. They can spot an IRA, a TSA, or a low-yield mutual fund fifty yards out. These people can wade their way through the muck of finance just fine, without hiring a professional.

But if you're like *most* people, after building your financial portfolio on your own for a bit, you get to a point where you don't have enough background to take you to the next level in financial wealth building.[1] It could be that you've recently started a business, need to find the best way to save for the kids' college, want to buy a home, aren't sure how to prepare for retirement, have come into a large sum of money, or perhaps, you're just really lonely. In cases like these, hiring a financial advisor might be in your best interest.

A financial advisor should be able to guide you in the direction you wish to head. Based on your goals, your timeline, your income and investments, as well as foreseen obstacles on your path, the right advisor should be able to offer you the assistance you need to get you as close to your goals as possible.

Now here's the funny thing. There are advisors for relationships too. There are marriage therapists, couples counselors, intimacy guides, and, I believe, even a Romance Guru based somewhere in

America. These people can help guide couples toward their relationship goals. Not every couple will need to hire a professional, but many will, and even more should but won't.

There are many reasons to hire a relationship professional as touched upon at the end of chapter three. Problems in the relationship is the most obvious reason:

- infidelity
- trust issues
- abuse
- constant arguing
- lack of communication
- sexual disconnect
- disrespect
- financial disagreement
- different child-rearing practices

But you can also see a professional for proactive reasons:

- expanding your sexual repertoire
- attending a couples' retreat to bring you closer
- taking a seminar to learn how to write a love letter
- having Mary Zalmanek come to your home to teach you Romantic Adventures skills (www.adventuresoftheheart .com)

## Avoiding Relationship Bankruptcy

What it really comes down to, whether you're being proactive or patching up the holes in your portfolio, is steering well clear of relationship bankruptcy. That's why folks look to financial professionals. They are avoiding financial bankruptcy.

Relationship bankruptcy is nothing more than the realization that your portfolio is empty. There's no romance left. The relationship no longer has legs to stand on. Where do you go next? You either live a cold, loveless existence, you cheat, or you file for Chapter 11 (divorce).

No sane individual or couple goes into a relationship hoping to eventually file for bankruptcy; seeing a professional is a smart and healthy option for many couples.

Remember there are many options. You can visit your professional regularly or make it a one-time, one-topic visit. You can go alone or as a couple. It can be a "repair" or just for "maintenance." You can find someone local or make it an adventure by going to a retreat, on a cruise, or attending a seminar/workshop.

You can start by reading articles and reports online or purchasing books such as this one. (Wow, I'm helping to build your relationship portfolio, and you're helping to build my financial portfolio! I'm sure we're going to be best friends.) At some sites, you can talk directly to a professional for free (like AllExperts.com) or for a small fee (like LivePerson.com). LiveAdvice.com offers services where you actually speak to someone over the phone. But most prefer that you meet and talk with a professional face-to-face.

You can find a professional by looking in your local phone book or from recommendations from people you trust. Some work places offer free or inexpensive professional assistance to their employees. A great place to start your search is the National Directory of Marriage and Family Counseling at www.counsel-search.com (refer to Resources, page 135, for more suggestions).

If you're looking for a professional to visit on a regular basis, *don't* feel you must stick with them. Though they might come highly recommended, have lots of degrees, and years of experience, relationship professionals are people like the rest of us. If you feel that you don't connect with one, it's your right to find another. You can't expect to open up if you don't connect with your counselor or therapist. And if you don't open up, you can't address your issues. If they are not being addressed, you're wasting everyone's time and not moving away from bankruptcy. So don't worry about offending a professional. It's *your* relationship. Find the counselor that works for you, and get the best bang for your buck.

## Heidi and Tom

Heidi and Tom had been together for nearly fifteen years, married for twelve, parents for nine. Since becoming parents, they noticed a change in their relationship. Nothing too intense. Sure, a little more bickering than before, but no real fights. No infidelity. Respect and trust were still there. No physical or verbal or emotional abuse. They were good parents and had sex about three times a month—less than the pre-parent years and very "white bread" (for those of you who don't know, that's an allusion to a plain white sandwich with mayo and a slice of bologna . . . not much pizzazz, very routine, and not very fulfilling).

What had changed significantly was communication and a decline in romance. The spark was gone. They felt like roommates in love that had separate lives; they were growing apart. Heidi and Tom were aware of this change. Neither blamed the other. They talked about how things had developed and decided to do something about it.

They brainstormed ideas: let's go on dates again, more sex, see a therapist, read a book on relationships together, and become more romantic. They decided to start with more romance. Tom would bring home flowers, and Heidi would surprise him with his favorite meal. Tom would email her an "I love you" at work, and Heidi would rub his shoulders on the sofa. They were going through the motions, but they really felt no change.

Next they added some dates into the mix. Although it was nice to get out, the couple really had forgotten how to communicate. So what do you do when you can't communicate? You guessed it—have sex! Tom and Heidi made it a point to have sex more often and at different times of the day and even in new locales.

This brought them out of their slump . . . temporarily. But after awhile the sex, albeit more often and in swivel chairs, became mundane as well. Tom was disillusioned and frustrated with all of this work and the lack of progress. Heidi suggested therapy or a book, once again. Tom explained that he felt going to a therapist made him feel like "a loser" or as though something was "wrong" with him. So he opted for the book. By this time Tom really wasn't feeling very motivated. His exuberance for restoring the spark in their relationship waned. All this work with no results had dampened his spirits.

Heidi chose a book, and the two started reading it together, but by halfway through Tom found other ways to occupy his time. He felt the book was just telling him to do the things he'd already tried that hadn't worked. To make matters worse, he had stopped doing those things.

The flowers and emails dwindled to a trickle. He initiated less dates, and sex was back to three times a month (on a good month . . . February was a "twice-a-month" month).

Heidi finished the book on her own, and she and Tom eventually separated, never having given a professional a shot to help them rebuild their portfolio before reaching bankruptcy. Looking back, Heidi wishes she had pushed more for the therapist, but didn't because, "Really, nothing was wrong." At least it felt that way, but obviously something was, and it doesn't look like they'll ever find the answers. Heidi could have gone to the therapist alone. Sure, it would be better to go as a couple, but had she gone alone, she may have received timely advice and much needed ammo for her "couple's arsenal" to bring back and use for target practice. Also it may have persuaded Tom into giving therapy a try.

You can't let pride or fear keep you from getting help when you need it. No one wants to lose what they've worked so hard for, and that includes love. Some couples will seek a professional in order to avoid a decline in their relationships. Others will get help when things start to get rocky. Still others will never use a professional and don't need to. But don't be the couple that waits too long and loses it all. You *deserve* your relationship.

## *Portfolio-Stretching Exercise*

1. Sit with your partner and openly discuss your relationship. Are there any problems that might constitute a reason to hire a professional? If so, skip to number six below. If not move on to number two.

2. If your relationship appears to be on solid ground, you have the choice to let the wind continue to take you on these calm waters for continuous smooth sailing, or to be proactive and add more to this already "good thing." If you want to keep sailing on your own, bon voyage, you are done. Move on to the next chapter. If you are considering a proactive approach, go down to step three.

3. Look at this list:
   - Books
   - Retreat/Cruise
   - One-on-one
   - Seminar
   - Sex

On separate sheets of paper write how you'd like to be proactive and add more if you'd like. If you are only interested in one topic, write it down. If you want to try more, write them across the top of your page with the one you're most interested in first. Below each one, list what you've heard of or might be interested in.

**Example:** Books

*Men are From Mars*

*101 Ways to Be Romantic*

*The Art of the Spark*

*Out of the Doghouse*

*The Finance of Romance* (hey, we're best friends, aren't we?)

4. Come together and compare lists. Any similarities? Anything on your partner's list you want to steal and add to yours?

5. Now discuss and determine where you want to start as a couple. Then jump right in. Now you may move to the next chapter.

6. What is the elephant in this relationship? What issue(s) is/are causing you to lose ground in your portfolio? Feel free to add to this list if your issue(s) is/are not listed:

| | | |
|---|---|---|
| Children/parenting | Infidelity | Trust |
| Substance Abuse | Sex | Emotional Abuse |
| Communication | Finances | Respect |

7. Write down all the issues you'd like resolved. Your partner will do the same. But do not share.

8. Look at your list and ask yourself what kind of professional you think would best help you. Again, if you think of a professional not listed, feel free to add to the list.

| | | |
|---|---|---|
| Psychologist | Couples' Therapist | Marriage Counselor |
| Lawyer | Financial Advisor | Intimacy Instructor |
| Doctor | Parenting/Family Coach | |

9. Now come together and, without getting too deep into the issue(s), discuss with your partner the type of professional you want to work with. In an ideal situation, you'll both agree on the help you need. Some compromising might be needed or you may actually need to seek assistance from more than one professional.

10. Either one of you can start the search, or you can work together. Feel free to use web searches, message boards, blogs, the phone book, personal referrals, or recommendations from work.

11. After setting your first appointment, but before arriving, look at your list of issues. For each one, write what you think is causing the rift. How do you feel? What would you like to see happen? It's nice having this list on hand when you arrive, so you'll have something to refer to in case your mind goes blank.

*ᴑᴆᴗ*

## *Key Points for Investing: Is It Time to Hire a Professional?*

✓ Many couples will use a professional to guide them through their portfolios.

✓ A professional can help when the portfolio is weakening.

✓ A professional can also help keep a healthy portfolio strong.

✓ The ultimate reason to hire a professional is to avoid bankruptcy.

✓ Some couples can avoid bankruptcy without help.

✓ If you realize there are stability issues, don't wait until it's too late.

✓ Once you choose a professional, you are not tied to them. If it's not a good match, find another.

## Note

1. *Getting The Facts of Saving and Investing*, US Securities Exchange Commission, 2007, 19.

— Chapter Twelve —

# WHEN TO CLOSE
# THE ACCOUNT

*Y*ou get an insider tip on an up and coming stock. You plunk down 5K ready for your investment to climb—but it doesn't at first. You see your initial investment shrinking ever so slightly to perhaps $4,500. You're thinking maybe it's just the market, but you notice other stocks are climbing. You decide you'll stick it out: $3,900. All stocks go through ups and downs, ebbs and flows: $3,300.

You're watching your capital disappear. Should you sell and walk away with a loss, or do you hang in there and pray for a turnaround: $2,700. You know that you're losing money, but by now you're financially *and* emotionally invested in this stock. You took a risk on this particular company because you believed in its potential. You believed the risk was worthwhile. You trusted that it would help your portfolio grow. Pulling out now can make you feel not only like you lost financially, but it can make you doubt yourself and your ability to choose wisely: $2,400. You're surely double-guessing yourself by now.

Yet you have the hope; maybe if you wait a little longer, the stock will turn around. But deep down, you know the chances for a rebound are pretty slim at this point. Everyone else's portfolios seem to be growing. But your choice in stock wasn't the right one: $1,900. You finally talk to your financial professional.

"Sell now, while you still have enough money to feed the parking meter." It's what you knew he would say. It's what you knew you should have done long ago. But you just needed that push, that outside voice of confirmation.

Disappointed with the stock, at your choice, and for waiting too long, you sell your shares and walk away with less than you started with, but with something you didn't have before: experience.

Experiences stay with us for a lifetime. If used correctly, they can help steer you clear of past mistakes and guide you to a brighter future. In essence they can be more valuable than $5,000 in stock.

To be honest, I wasn't too excited about writing this chapter, but it is very important with regard to investing in your relationship portfolio. I sure as heck hope that the investing tips you've already read and have been following—hint, hint—keep you from having to close your account. However, the reality is no book will save every relationship. And it's important that we cover this possibility as well.

You fall in love, date, get engaged, and maybe even tie the knot; it's probably the biggest risk you've taken in life, but one that you feel most confident in. Love, truly loving someone, is giving your heart to another, handing them your emotions, and trusting another to care for them. When you fall in love fully, you expose your heart and feelings. You hope to Mt. Olympus that they don't fall victim to frost bite.

## Worth the Risk?

Why do we invest in relationships? Why would we risk having our emotions trampled and our relationship dreams destroyed? Because the potential benefits far outweigh the risks. The love, commitment, passion, reliability, safety, friendship, family, intimacy, partnership, desire, security, companionship, trust, and patience are what we all desire. And we know that to truly experience them, we need to put our investment at risk. If we invest in a stock that shoots to the moon, it was all worth it. But if we buy one that tanks, we're crushed!

You put yourself out there and it feels right at first, but at some point something changes. You see the drop in your relationship investment. The risk factor increases. You understand that all relationships have hills and valleys, and you hope to stay the course. But things get worse. There's more arguing. Less sex. A lack of communication. You are growing apart from one another.

It's a hard pill to swallow, thinking that the relationship won't work. Maybe you try the techniques in this book: you date, you play hooky, you find more time for communication. Maybe you even seek professional support.

Nothing's helping, and you know it. You feel it, but you don't want to admit it. It's frustrating and maddening. You get mad at your partner, your situation (stress at work, parenthood, financial problems), and even at yourself for being so naïve, making such a dumb mistake, or not trying hard enough. In reality, there are times when no one is to blame, like when you're the fastest runner, but you're not allowed to win (think Howard Jones).

You think that maybe if you wait long enough things will get better on their own—like your car. Sometimes your car won't start, so you walk away, come back ten minutes later and give it a try, and the engine turns over. If it works for your Fiat, why not for your relationship, right?

We do this because we've invested so much into this particular relationship portfolio, into this fund, this stock. We don't want to pull out and be left with far less than we initially invested.

It's a tough choice to make, but sometimes it's inevitable. It's hard because you look back and see that you've wasted so much. Your heart is broken. Your emotions are frayed. The time you spent on the relationship is time you can't get back, time you may think would have been better spent single or with another partner.

So why not just stay with your initial investment and hope it will flip? I mean, isn't closing the account guaranteeing bankruptcy? Sticking it out can't be worse, can it? Yes, it can (and will) be worse.

If you have exhausted all attempts at getting this portfolio to grow—if there really is no life left in the relationship—you could just watch your investment dwindle to nothing, and you wouldn't be the first.

## Staying When You Shouldn't

Some couples will stay together when they know they've crossed the point of no return. The slippery slope becomes too steep to climb, but they don't want to hurt the children, disappoint family, or go against their faith. Even though they're unhappy, they're also comfortable.

That's a strange one, but so very prevalent. Often we will stay in situations that make us unhappy because they are convenient—they are what we know and are comfortable. To move out of our comfort zone takes work, and many times we're more afraid of the unknown than we are of the unhappiness we're all too familiar with.

No matter the reason, if couples stay in relationships whose portfolios have no chance of rebounding, they will reach bankruptcy. Bankruptcy is wrought with anger, frustration, depression, and resentment. Couples may actually begin to hate each other, their relationship, their lives—even themselves. A bankrupt relationship can, and most likely will, affect work, family, and friends.

These couples just exist day-by-day, wondering what life would have been like had they made other choices. In these relationships, often one or both partners stray. These relationships often include abuse, verbal, emotional, and even physical. Although closing the account comes with it's own con list, waiting for bankruptcy is far worse.

Let me reiterate (as if you have any control on my iterating or my re-iterating), I am not advocating bailing on a relationship when you hit a rough patch. If you are in a long-term, committed relationship, odds are you can work through the dips that all relationships encounter. Granted, you take care of things early on, or better yet, you're proactive and avoid as many obstacles as you can. I only advocate closing the account when all other attempts to salvage the relationship have been exhausted.

## Benefiting from Closing the Account

Just like selling your shares of a stock that went belly-up, if you're willing, you can learn from your experience. Most couples leave a relationship seeing only the negative, thinking they wasted time and emotion. Later on, many look back and realize the experience was another step that helped them be closer to where they wanted to be in life.

Relationships that go bankrupt can actually teach us how to love—if we focus on the positive experiences and memories. We also learn what worked and didn't work in the partnership. We discover what we really want in a partner and what we don't. We have the opportunity to learn more about ourselves and to discover what we need to change to be a better partner. We understand how to protect ourselves and what our vulnerabilities are. And, if we're wise, when we are ready we can take all of what we learn to our next relationship.

Here's the part that sounds nuttier than a can of Planter's Cocktail Mix: we may even eventually appreciate the fallen relationship and may thank our ex for helping us reach a new level of love with someone else.

## Brenda and Aaron

I'd met Brenda and Aaron during their sixth year of marriage. She was the office receptionist at a dental clinic, and he worked for the forestry service. Brenda was a sweet, conservative woman and a bit on the quiet side, somewhat an introvert. She was originally from Chile and spoke with a heavy accent. Aaron, seven years Brenda's junior, was out-going and gregarious. He worked for the forestry service cleaning brush and cutting back overgrown and downed trees.

By all accounts the two appeared happy. They owned a modest home and seemed to be always working on it: redoing the kitchen, mason work in the backyard, landscaping. Their home was beautiful. They had no children, but treated their three cats, Larry, Curly and Mark, as if they were their offspring.

Brenda and Aaron proudly entertained guests at their home—barbecues in the backyard, holiday parties inside. They took pride in their home and their lifestyle. As life continued, Aaron started his own tree-trimming business and spent much of his time building his "empire," a venture that Brenda supported.

About four years after meeting the couple, I learned there were many speed bumps on their racetrack of marriage, which were hindering a smooth ride to their finish line. They asked if I could offer some support; they both wanted the relationship to work out.

We looked at all possibilities: time spent together, communication, bringing romance back, going out on dates. The couple attended one of my seminars. I gave both of them books to read. They were genuinely trying to find a way to get their relationship back on track!

Eventually they found a couple's therapist who they met with regularly as a couple and also individually. In the meantime, communication was labored between the two. Aaron spent more time at his business. Intimacy stopped, and the couple was sleeping in separate rooms. Their portfolio was riddled with holes, and they were quickly losing ground on their initial investment.

After eighteen months of trying to keep the investment afloat, Aaron and Brenda officially closed their account. They separated and eventually divorced. Sure it was difficult, exhausting, and emotional, but they both knew holding on to a failing investment would have lead to relationship bankruptcy, which would have been far worse.

They definitely were angry and frustrated and had the feeling of "Look at all the years we've lost" at first, but slowly both learned to appreciate their ten years' experience together. Brenda is taking time to discover who she really is and how she's grown as an individual through her relationship with Aaron. Aaron has decided to take time off from serious relationships. He enjoys meeting women and flirting but has turned his focus to building his business. Both will be better partners when they enter into new relationships, because of the lessons learned from their first investment.

At times, it's best to walk away from a loss. If you play poker, you can only sit there so long with a bad hand and continue to call the bets (just like Kenny Rogers sings about in "The Gambler"). Eventually you must fold a bad hand, because if you hold out too long, your chip pile gets obliterated.

When multi-gazillionaire Warren Buffett was a teen, he lost a bet at the race track. To recoup his loss, he bet on another race and lost yet again. He left the track broke that day. He felt frustrated and sick, but he learned a valuable lesson: know when to quit. He never repeated this mistake again.[1] You can only really learn those types of lessons from experience. One day at the track and a week's worth of lost wages was a great investment that helped Buffett the rest of his life.

If you need to close your relationship account, use the experience to become a better person. Take lessons from the partnership. Find your mistakes and vow to never repeat them.

# *Portfolio-Stretching Exercise*

1. If you're feeling frustrated with your partner and disillusioned in your relationship, take a step back and ask yourself how long you've felt this way. Has this happened before? Are you generally happy with the relationship or unhappy? You don't need to share this with your partner just yet, but if you feel as though you're "stuck" in this relationship, that you have found yourself less than happy as a direct result of the relationship—and this has been going on for at least six months—there's probably a real problem here.

2. What is it precisely that frustrates you? Bickering? Trust issues? Communication? Loss of chemistry? What is it? Create a list with specific examples.

3. Once you have figured out what is distracting you from your partner, talk to him or her. This can often be the most difficult part of the process, but it's *integral* to helping you through. Go back to chapter three and practice using the "I" statements. You don't want to accuse, attack, or make your partner feel as though he or she needs to get defensive or put on the boxing gloves. What you're trying to do is lay it all out so your partner will feel comfortable doing the same.

4. After your partner has listened to you—and they will only listen if you don't accuse them—ask for their perspective. *Listen* to what they're saying; don't interrupt or defend yourself.

5. With everything verbalized, it's time to discuss where you want to go as a couple. Of course, the goal should be to resolve your issues. Depending upon what they are, you may need a support group, learn to communicate better and in positive ways, or apply advice from this book or others. Or maybe it's time to seek out a professional.

6. If you have exhausted all avenues of reconciliation, if you're still frustrated, depressed, or angry, if you dread coming home

to your partner, and your energy is being zapped by this exhausting relationship, you may be losing your investment, and it's probably time to talk to one another, as well as your relationship professional, about possible separation or divorce.

A lot is involved with separating two lives that have been interwoven over many years (for some). This chapter cannot do justice to the difficulty of going separate ways. That's why communicating with one another as well as with a third party (the professional) is so crucial.

◯◯◯

## *Key Points for Investing: When to Close the Account*

✓ Sometimes an investment is draining you too much, and you need to cut your losses.

✓ If you don't, it could bankrupt you.

✓ There are risks in relationships.

✓ We take these risks because the benefits outweigh the negatives.

✓ Yet, the risks remain.

✓ Closing an account feels like a loss, but learning from the experience is the best way to handle the loss.

✓ Use the knowledge gained from your "loss" to help avoid repeating the same mistakes.

**Note**

1. Warren Buffett, "10 Ways to Get Rich," *Parade Magazine*, Sept. 7, 2008, 5–6.

— Chapter Thirteen —

# HITTING THE LOTTERY

$\mathcal{T}$here's nothing wrong with playing the lottery now and again. A scratcher here, Mega Power Ball there. Someone's got to win, right? Might as well be you. Can't win if you don't play. Odds are something like one in eleven million that you'll hit the big one, the life-changing grand prize, the "oh-what-the-heck, I think I will supersize my meal" windfall.

But don't count on it.

We can't truly rely on hitting the lottery as a means, a *plan*, to take care of all of our financial obligations. There has to be a Plan B . . . and C and D. Like, for instance—oh, I don't know—maybe, get a job! That would be a reasonable place to start if for some reason your "quick picks" fell short this week. You also might consider a savings account, maybe investing—the stuff this book is full of.

As long as you know that you've got a back-up plan, go ahead and play the lottery every once in awhile. I mean, look at me. I do it. I've been playing the same six numbers twice a week for the last twenty years, which makes my odds even better. Now, I'm somewhere close to 10,998, 000 to 1. At this rate I'm pretty much guaranteed to hit it by the time I'm 11,041 years old . . . like I'd have the chonies to enjoy the cash at that age.

I play the lottery because it's fun to dream. I know my odds are slim, but I also know that my odds would be zilch if I didn't play.

That sliver of possibility is fun for me. It allows me to dream and ask, "What if?" Dreaming is good for us; it gets us thinking outside of our current conditions. We stretch and sometimes find ourselves closer to our dreams, because thoughts lead to belief, and belief leads to action, and action leads to change.

I would hope that your financial advisor would not discourage you from playing the lottery every so often. As long as you're not investing a week's pay, or banking on it as your sole means toward financial freedom, your financial advisor should tell you to have fun. If by chance you did hit it big, your advisor would be licking her chops—what with all of your winnings to invest, which would mean commissions for her. (And don't forget about me; I'm the one who told you to buy that winning ticket!) So, go on. Have fun!

## All Your Worries Gone . . . Right?

But what the pork and beans does this have to do with relationships? When you hit the actual lottery, you're set financially, right? All your money problems are gone. And you can sail smoothly the rest of the way on this clear-as-glass lake called "life."

In the same way, when you hit the relationship lottery, you've hit the jackpot. There are no bumps in your road. Love feels great. Romance and passion are prevalent. Communication between the two of you is perfectly balanced. Arguments are disagreements you've seen on Fox sitcoms and things that other couples experience. There's trust and respect. Mistakes (the few that arise) are easily and quickly forgiven. Your car runs on water and your dog never sheds. It's the utopian Shangri-la of relationships—and just like Shangri-la, it doesn't exist.

Sorry.

I don't mean to be the one to burst your pumpkin, but there is no perfect relationship. All relationships experience some turbulence if the flight is long enough. That's because relationships are dynamic, not static. They are in constant flux, because we're always changing (see chapter four). Even if you follow the guidelines of this book and change together as a couple, there will still be deviation, and that deviation causes rifts, and rifts make Shangri-la impossible.

So what's all this rubbish about striving for hitting the relationship lottery? It's an idea that's out there and it's good to try for the Mega Power Ball. But like the actual lottery, know that you probably won't hit it. Instead of being disappointed that your relationship isn't like June and Ward Cleaver's (although, I can't imagine Beaver's mom exploring new ways to keep intimacy exciting), revel in the little wins that you come by.

I have never won the Super Lottery, but I have hit three numbers at times. That's a surprise five or ten bucks every now and again. It's not life-changing, but it's a win that I can celebrate. Then I buy another ticket and try again the next week.

## Small Victories

You may not hit the perfect relationship, but you can appreciate the small wins and the parts that are working well. Keep working toward hitting all six numbers. Having the perfect relationship is virtually impossible, so invest the small wins back into your relationship, and it will grow and reap more dividends. Know that when your port-folio grows, it brings to you a better chance of more wins and more opportunities to build your portfolio. And with a growing portfolio, relationship bankruptcy will never loom on the horizon.

Keep in mind that of the one-in-eleven-million who do win the big money, most end up throwing it all away. I recall reading some-where (*Reader's Digest* or a Superman comic book) that something like 70 percent of lottery jackpot winners go broke within five years after hitting it big. Why?

Because they stop making sound financial decisions.

They feel that the good times will last forever. They spend frivo-lously and stop investing wisely. You can't do that in your relation-ship. No matter how great the relationship is, you need to continue to work to keep it great. Don't sit back on your haunches. Don't put it on cruise control. Don't assume the relationship will take care of itself. It needs you, both of you, and your continuous efforts and diversification, your good credit.

## Jacob's Folks

When I was in high school, a kid named Jacob had a stay-at-home mom and a dad who owned a construction company and coached the school football team. When Jacob's grandfather died, the family was left something like nine million dollars. This was in the mid-eighties, so that's a little over eighteen million dollars in today's economy.

Well, Jacob's family became the Rockefellers of our little California mountain community: BMWs, 24-hour limo service, and a beautiful home in a gated community. They even bought a TV/movie studio.

Man, I thought that these guys were so lucky! They had it all: money, toys, big house, Kellogg's cereal instead of the store brand—everything.

While I was in college, I learned that Jacob's family had spent their inheritance. The house was sold. The limousine service was cancelled. The movie studio was foreclosed (with not even one Beta movie being released). Dad was back in construction and coaching. Fruity Ohs rather than Fruit Loops. But most disappointing was that Jacob's parents had divorced.

Not only had they failed in growing their financial portfolio, but as a result of the money, toys, and the distractions, they abandoned their relationship portfolio completely.

Hitting the jackpot is a wonderful dream; it helps us to visualize how we'd like to live our future. And for many, it helps to take steps in that direction. But we must always remember, be it money or love, we must *do*. We must work. We must put out effort if we expect a return.

Love, like money, is no good without someone taking care of it and fostering it and helping it grow. That someone is you!

## *Portfolio-Stretching Exercise*
(See Worksheet 11)

1. Set aside some time together to discuss the "perfect relationship." What would that mean? Time together? Time alone? Traveling? Going out to dinner? Dates? More sex? Less sex? What about communication? How about household duties and parenting? Discuss what winning the relationship jackpot

would mean to you, and write down the items you both agree on. Brainstorm. Go wild. It can be as simple as saying "I love you" every morning, or skinny-dipping in the neighbor's pool every night. It can be as silly as role-playing "pizza delivery boy and cougar" or as serious as no more physical abuse.

2. It's important that you discuss what you see as the perfect relationship. You may mention something your partner never thought of, but would agree with. If you have slightly differing views on a topic, it's okay to compromise so both parties are reasonably satisfied. But if you have polar opposite views ("I want to snuggle more each night," "I'd like separate beds"), then just leave it off the list.

3. Take your time. Once you have your list, let it sit on the kitchen counter for twenty-four hours. Inevitably, thoughts will pop into your heads that you'll want to add to the list. Discuss and, if appropriate, add it.

4. After your twenty-four hour window, post the list on your fridge (unless it mentions deviant sex in gorilla outfits . . . wouldn't want the Hendersons to read that at the next 4H club meeting), on your bathroom mirror, your closet door, or maybe a dresser drawer you both access.

5. Before you stick it away or post it up, choose one item on the list you two will strive to do for a month to get your relationship that much closer to "perfect." Make it a priority for thirty days. Talk together about what it takes to make this a reality.

6. After the month is over, assess your progress. (This would be very convenient to do on the same day you wrote down monthly dates). Did you reach your goal? Is your relationship stronger? If not, what needs to be tweaked: the path to reaching the goal, or the goal itself? Make adjustments and try again.

7. If you have reached the goal, reinvest by continuing to do what you are doing. You don't want to lose this new relationship strategy. Now, choose another item on the list to invest in.

Rinse and repeat. Do it again. Keep working at this, and you'll be taking baby steps toward "the perfect relationship."

8. By the way, you can both change your list along the way. If you both agree to add more items, do so. If there are items that no longer reflect what you are striving for in a relationship, delete them. If there are items that need to be updated, make the appropriate changes. Who knows; you may achieve Shangri-la.

*Key Points for Investing:*
*Hitting the Lottery*

✓ There's nothing wrong with trying to win "the jackpot."

✓ Setting goals and dreaming big is important in finance, relationships, and other aspects of life.

✓ The reality, though, is that no relationship is perfect.

✓ Celebrate the small victories.

✓ It takes work to achieve our relationship goals; relationships don't grow on trees.

✓ Only you can foster love in your relationship and help it to grow.

✓ I guarantee that the work you put into your relationship now is an investment that will reap incredible dividends down the road.

*Keep spinning.*

— Appendix—

# WORKSHEETS, RESOURCES, & OTHER ACTIVITIES

# — WORKSHEET ONE —

*Use with the "Portfolio-Stretching Exercise" in Chapter 1*

## My Top Priorities This Week

Name_____     Date_____

1.

2.

3.

4.

5.

6.

7.

8.

**Notes:**

_____

_____

_____

_____

_____

_____

_____

_____

# — WORKSHEET TWO —

*Use with the "Portfolio-Stretching Exercise" in Chapter 1*

## My Ideal Top Priorities This Week

Name_____          Date_____

1.

2.

3.

4.

5.

6.

7.

8.

**Notes:**

_____

_____

_____

_____

_____

_____

_____

## — Worksheet Three —

*Use with the "Portfolio-Stretching Exercise" in Chapter 1*

# Our Ideal Top Priorities This Week

Names_____     .     Date_____

1.

2.

3.

4.

5.

## What We Need to Do to Make These Realities

•

•

•

•

•

*Use with the "Portfolio-Stretching Exercise" in Chapter 2*

## Relationship Goal

_____

_____

## Ways to Reach the Goal

1.

2.

3.

I want _____,

therefore I resolve that I will _____

_____

_____.

"My_____ Resolution"

*Use with the "Portfolio-Stretching Exercise" in Chapter 2*

## Relationship Goal

_____

_____

## Ways to Reach the Goal

1.

2.

3.

I want _____,

therefore I resolve that I will _____

_____

_____.

"My_____ Resolution"

*Use with the "Portfolio-Stretching Exercise" in Chapter 3*

## Obstacles Leading to Debt

-
-
-

### Obstacles      Emotions

-
-
-

*Use with the "Portfolio-Stretching Exercise" in Chapter 3*

## The Obstacle

_____

_____

## What I Really Want to Say about It

_____

_____

_____

_____

_____

_____

_____

_____

_____

_____

_____

_____

_____

# — WORKSHEET EIGHT —

*Use with the "Portfolio-Stretching Exercise" in Chapter 3*

## The "I" Statement

I feel _____

when you _____

because _____

_____.

I want _____.

**The Goal:**

_____

_____

_____

_____

_____

_____

_____

# Our "Risk List"

**Examples:**

- ride thrill rides at a local amusement park
- have sex in the backyard
- go river rafting
- rock climbing
- bungee jumping

**Add Your Own:**

- 
- 
- 
- 
- 
- 
- 
- 
- 
- 
-

*Use with the "Portfolio-Stretching Exercise" in Chapter 8*

# Where I'd Like to See Some Changes in Our Sex Life

*Check off the areas you are interested in changing.*
*If an area is not listed, list your own in the blanks.*
*Below each one, list the changes you would like to see.*

☐ Foreplay                    ☐ Role-playing

☐ Length of Session           ☐ Frequency

☐ Location                    ☐ Racy Literature

☐ Toys                        ☐ Time of Day

☐ Visual Stimulation          ☐ _____

☐ _____                 ☐ _____

*Use with the "Portfolio-Stretching Exercise" in Chapter 13*

## Hitting The Relationship Jackpot

*List ways you both agree on to create the "perfect relationship"*

- 
- 
- 
- 
- 
- 
- 

*Choose one of the items from the list and focus on it
for the next thirty days.*

## After the month:

- Did you reach your goal?
- Is your relationship better?
- If not, what needs to be tweaked: the path to reaching the goal, or the goal itself?
- Make adjustments and try again.

— Resources —

*Use in conjunction with Chapter 11*

## Resources for Finding
## a Relationship Professional

- aamft.org
  *The American Association for Marriage and Family Therapy*

- counsel-search.com
  *The National Directory for Marriage & Family Counseling*

- family-marriage-counseling.com
  *The Family & Marriage Counseling Directory*

- fixmyfamily.com
  *Marriage Counseling, Family Therapy Directory and Resources*

- relationshipresourcecenter.com
  *The Relationship Resource Center*

- therelationshipinstitute.org/resources-marriage-counseling-information.html
  *The Relationship Institute*

# — Websites —

*Websites to Help Invest in Your Relationship*

- sms3insb.com (Chapter 4)—to order the *Word-Up*, Verbal "Notes" for Reconnecting

- MemoToMe.com (Chapter 5)—date reminders

- DebtProofLiving.com (Chapter 6)—Mary Hunt's Financial Help

- GetRichSlowly.com (Chapter 8)—JD Roth's Financial Blog

- TraceyCox.com (Chapter 8)—clever ways to improve your sex life

- MaddiesMonkeyBusiness.com (Chapter 10)—twelve-year-old's inspirational business site

- AdventuresOfTheHeart.com (Chapter 11)—romantic adventures

- counsel-search.com (Chapter 11)—marriage and family counselors' search

- AllExperts.com (Chapter 11)—find an expert in any field for free

- LivePerson.com (Chapter 11)—get real time help online for a small fee

# — Books —

*Books to Help Invest in Your Relationship*

- **101 Nights of Grrreat Sex** (Laura Corn—creative ways to keep excitement in the bedroom)

- **1001 Ways to Be Romantic** (Greg Godek—the title says it all)

- **A Labor with Love: A Dad's-to-Be Guide to Romance During Pregnancy** (Leon Scott Baxter—keeping romance alive during pregnancy)

- **Art of the Spark** (Mary Zalmanek—guide for creating romantic adventures)

- **The Five Love Languages** (Gary Chapman—helps couples interpret partner's ideas of "love")

- **Love Her Right: The Married Man's Guide to Lesbian Secrets for Great Sex** (Dr. Joni Frater, Esther Lastique)

- **Out of the Doghouse: A Man's Secret Survival Guide to Romance** (Leon Scott Baxter—A man's Cliffs Notes to relationship survival)

- **The Mars & Venus Diet & Exercise Solution** (John Gray—create the brain chemistry of lasting romance)

- **Men: A Translation for Women** (Joan Shapiro—Ladies, have you always wondered what he was thinking?)

- **Superhotsex** (Tracey Cox—Again, the title says it all)

# — Extra Activity 1 —

*Here's a Portfolio Stretching-Exercise not mentioned in the thirteen chapters of the book, but it's a great complement to chapter 6. Find a way to squeeze this one in.*

# Dating Decisions

If you are tired of making all the date decisions but are the only one who will show any dating initiative, here's the perfect date for you.

Send your sweetheart an invitation for a date. However, create the options in multi-choice so they have to make the decision for once. Here's an example (be sure to create your own):

Let's go out for dinner on:
___ Thursday
___ Friday
___ Saturday
___ Sunday

at:
___ Burger King
___ Waffle House
___ The Shiny Diner
___ Maldonado's

followed by:
___ Playing on the swings in the park
___ A jazz concert
___ An air hockey competition at the arcade
___ A banana split at the malt shop

This creative activity was furnished by Michael Webb from www.TheRomantic.com. Check out his site for more great ideas.

*Here's a Portfolio Stretching-Exercise not mentioned in the thirteen chapters of the book, but it's a great complement to chapters 3 and 4. Find a way to squeeze this one in.*

# Say It Now

Too often, when we lose someone we think of everything we loved about them, the qualities we'll miss, and we wish we had told them when they were still with us. It happens all the time, but it was on such a grand scale when we lost Michael Jackson in 2009.

He'd been ridiculed, parodied, and become the butt of so many jokes during his life, but when he left us, we showed how much we truly loved him and would miss him, and that got me thinking that Michael really didn't know how much we cared for him during the second part of his life. I'm sure he would have loved to know while he was still with us.

For this activity, what would you have wished to say to your partner if they died? (Don't get too morbid!) Write down the great memories, what you love about them, secrets you wish you had told them. Describe what made them your soul mate and how fortunate you have been to have them in your life.

Now, change all of that to the present tense, and tell your partner today . . . while she is still breathing. Don't be embarrassed to open your heart. Let her know today how you feel so you won't regret not telling her tomorrow.

# — Extra Activity 3 —

*Here's a Portfolio-Stretching Exercise not mentioned in the thirteen chapters of the book, but it's a great complement to chapters 3 and 4. Find a way to squeeze this one in.*

## Tell It Like It Is

This is a relatively simple activity to open up the lines of communication between you and your partner. Go to separate rooms and finish these two sentences:

1. Romance is _____.
2. Love is _____.

Before you run off and "fill in the blank" like this is some junior high school pop quiz, *think* about your answers before writing them down. And feel free to go into depth in your answer. Don't just stick a word or two in the blank.

When you both have completed the assignment, come together and share what you've written. There is no right or wrong answer here (unless, of course, you've really choked on this quiz and your partner sets the curve). "So, what's the point?" I'm glad you asked!

Sometimes it's a real eye-opener to learn what your partner sees as love and romance. Don't let this be a catalyst for an argument. Use it to learn more about each other and get closer to your relationship goals.

## — EXTRA ACTIVITY 4 —

*Here's a Portfolio Stretching-Activity not mentioned in the thirteen chapters of the book, but it's a great complement to chapters 3 and 4. Find a way to squeeze this one in.*

# To Tell the Truth

This is a fun, short quiz for you to get to know your partner a little better. You both get a piece of paper. One of you reads the question and you both write your answer. When done, go on to the next question. When you complete all ten, share what you wrote with each other.

- If you won a million dollars on a reality show, but couldn't spend the money on yourself, what would you do with it?
- Have you ever done anything really risky? If so, what?
- If you could go anywhere in the world, where would it be and why there?
- If you could only choose to be one of the following, which would you pick: smart, rich, attractive, funny, or well-known?
- If you had a time machine and could change any event in history, what would you change and why?
- What if you could use that time machine to change your own history, would you do it? If so, what would you change and why?
- What's the most embarrassing thing that has happened to you?
- What skill or talent do you wish you could master?
- What non-fiction character are you most like?
- In which way(s) would you like to be more like me? (Not *me*; your partner!)

## — EXTRA ACTIVITY 5 —

*Here's a Portfolio-Stretching Exercises not mentioned in the thirteen chapters of the book, but it's a great complement to chapter 3. Find a way to squeeze this one in.*

## Talk It Out

Something we rarely do in our relationships in our society is to sit down and talk about our goals and concerns. If it ain't broke, why fix it, right? Well, knowing we're walking on the path in the same direction as well as voicing our concerns *before* they become problems are wise moves to make, and this exercise will help.

**Make a list of your top three relationship goals:**

_____

_____

_____

**Make a list of your top three relationship concerns:**

_____

_____

_____

Exchange your lists with each other, and use them as a discussion starter and to begin moving closer to a common relationship experience.

One more thing: take the top concern from each of your lists and together think of at least one concrete thing you can do to make this concern less . . . concerning. Once you have it, start working on it. (By the way, once you have the top concern under wraps, you could always shoot for concern #2 . . . just an idea.)

# — RELATIONSHIP BUCKS —

Since we're talking about finance and romance, what better way to tie the two together than with Relationship Bucks. I've included templates for a one- and five-dollar bill on the next page. Make a copy, and stick your face in the center. Then become your own Treasury Department and print off as much "money" as you like (but don't go overboard; that's how inflation starts). There's also a great site where you can make even cooler, more realistic moolah (www.festisite.com/money/).

## How to Use the Relationship Bucks

Simple. Print up a couple hundred bucks or so for your own little economy. Then figure out together how to get that money into the "public" (in both of your hands). Make a list you agree on together: five bucks for doing the bills; a ten spot for washing the laundry; a Jackson for washing dishes; whatever you choose. When one of you "earns" your cash, you take it from the bank, until all of the money is in your hands.

Next figure out how you can spend it. Each of you decide how much you will pay your partner for an act: a dollar a kiss; five bucks for a neck massage; ten dollars to let me watch the game with no interruptions; twenty-five dollars for that thing you do with the Slip N' Slide and the baby oil. You can use the list in chapter 10 to get you started.

Let the money flow back and forth between you. If you want to change either list, go for it. If you find that there's not enough cash in your economy either lower your price list, or print some more dough.

# — Coupons —

What frugal-minded investor would pass up the opportunity to use investment coupons? Trading coupons with your partner is a fun and creative way to keep romance alive in your relationship, while also learning what your partner thinks you want.

Write out a few coupons using the template below or go to www.romancestuck.com/custom/love-coupons/love-coupon-creator.htm and create your own online. Staple the coupons together to make a "Coupon Book." Hand it to your partner and get ready to redeem your coupons.

## Relationship Coupon

This coupon good for:

_____

_____

_____

Love, _____

(no expiration date)

# ACKNOWLEDGMENTS

The acknowledgments page of a book is not much unlike the acceptance speech of an Academy Award winner: "I'd like to thank my mom and the producers, and none of this would have been possible without God Almighty."

Thing is, since having written this book and knowing that I would be offering shout-outs to all who helped make it possible, I've been studying Academy Awards acceptance speeches, what works, and what doesn't. Who to thank first and who gets the snub. I've also gauged my reaction to said speeches, and the first thing I noticed was that I tend to listen to the beginning of these acknowledgments, but if I don't know who the lighting director was and who the incredible head of wardrobe is, my mind drifts halfway through the thing.

So, I've learned that I need to mention right here up front the most important entity and my biggest inspiration—my wife, Mary. Without her, I wouldn't know the true, deep, and profound love I try to help others experience. Mary has always been in my corner and I count myself blessed to get to wake up to her every morning.

This book would never have come to exist had it not been for Ocean Hills Covenant Church in Santa Barbara, who invited me to do a Valentine's Day talk that eventually became *The Finance of Romance*.

Without my scanners (as I call them), this book wouldn't be what it is today. The following folks read draft after draft, offered insights and comments. I so appreciate their opinions and judgment: Dr. Joni Frater & Esther Lastique, Elizabeth Blake, Gary Spinell, Talayah Stovall, D. E. Boone, Judy Helm Wright, Gary Patterson (the Fiscal Doctor), Steve Nakamoto (Mr. Answer Man), Gail Rubin, Susan Heim, Mary Zalmanek, and Paul & Debbie Lamb.

I want to offer special thanks to my close friend and finance wizard, Tim Tremblay, for his time, advice, and guidance, with the finance part of *The Finance of Romance.* Another special thanks goes to Michael Webb, "The Romantic," who knows how to help men keep their partners interested. I can't forget talk show host Line Brunet, who believes so highly in this book's concept. She is one of my biggest cheerleaders, and I look forward to working with her in the future.

Simon Presland was a gift sent to me directly from the heavens. With his dry wit and dedication to precision, Simon was the ultimate book editor, catching my typos and ill-command of English grammar, making me appear to be a bit more literate than I truly am. I stumbled across this incredible man and would recommend him as an editor to anyone who wants a book that is coherent and a colleague who will offer honest feedback while making you smile. Look him up at www.thewritechoice.org.

If it weren't for my agent, Mary Sue Seymour, I probably would never have been connected with the wonderful folks at Cedar Fort, Inc., who have taken a very special interest in *The Finance of Romance.* Managing editor, Heather Holm, and acquisitions editor Shersta Gatica were the first two I met at Cedar Fort and they represented the company in a manner that made me feel relaxed and at home. Marketing publicist Mariah Overlook, has been the one that has helped me go from writer to marketer. And my editor, Melissa Caldwell, has guided me through commas and typos in a way less like third grade student and teacher and more like, well, a seventh grade teacher and student—she's been great!

Another thing I learned studying Oscar acceptance speeches is that if the statue recipient has not bored the audience with his long list of thank-yous, the last acknowledgment is nearly as important as the first. So, for those of you who have made it this far, I would like to offer my final thank you to the late Dom DeLuise. No, not for the Cannonball Run movies (although they did help me through the '80s), but because early on in life I learned romance from the comic legend.

I was in college working the front desk at an all-suites hotel just outside of Santa Barbara, CA. Dom's wife, Carol Arthur, was in town for a month playing Miss Hannigan in a local production of Little Orphan Annie. She stayed at our property and every single day for that month, an envelope came for her from Dom, and every night, like clockwork, at 8:45 he would call to speak with her. If she wasn't in, he and I would chat and we eventually became phone buddies.

On closing night of the play, Dom came to his wife's show and asked to meet me. He was a rather large man, not someone one would think of when you heard the word romantic. Yet when I saw the love in his and Carol's eyes, it was the first time I truly understood what romance was. It wasn't what you did for your partner, but rather how you made your partner feel. Dom's calls, cards, and smiles made Carol feel loved and cared for. That is romance. Thank you, Dom.

# ABOUT THE AUTHOR

$\mathcal{L}$eon Scott Baxter, "America's Romance Guru" is the author of *Out of the Doghouse: A Man's Secret Survival Guide to Romance* and *A Labor with Love.* He's spoken to over 20,000 people about love and relationships. His website, CouplesCommittedToLove.com, allows visitors to access his book, articles, reports, seminars and phone coaching.

Baxter has been a guest on radio and podcast programs, locally and internationally. He blogs regularly about how popular culture affects relationships, and is a regular guest on the A.M. radio show, "Talking with America." He has answered nearly 2,000 inquiries as an expert on relationships at AllExperts.com, and is one of the most popular in his field of expertise.

Leon Scott Baxter lives in Southern California with his college sweetheart, Mary—who he has been married to since 1992—his two beautiful daughters, Madison and Maya, and his Boxer/Terrier mix, Lucy. He enjoys playing basketball, skimboarding, and watching reruns of the hit TV series *The A-Team.*

# Lucky You!

As a thank-you for reading *The Finance of Romance*, I want to offer you another of my books for free . . . really, no strings attached (I wouldn't lie to you).

## *Out of the Doghouse: A Man's Secret Survival Guide to Romance*

*Out of the Doghouse* is a fun and easy-to-use cheat sheet for romance. It's the Cliff's Notes to love. A man can use it to find poems, love letters, romantic music, passionate adventures, and reproducible pages for nearly any romantic event. The information is offered in bite-size man chunks and comes with a quick reference guide to make last-minute romantic decisions a snap.

To receive your free electronic version of *Out of the Doghouse* ($14.99 value), please head over to CouplesCommitted-ToLove.com and click on the "Get Book Free" button. Just use the promo code "FINANCE" to get a copy of *Out of the Doghouse* emailed directly to you.